TO

FROM

GOSPEL NOTES

-FOR-

ATHEISTS, CLERGY, HEATHEN,
NERDS, POLITICIANS, REDNECKS,
&
SCIENTISTS

VOLUME II

FRED J. STONE

Scripture references are from the Revised Standard Version of 1952 unless otherwise indicated.

Cover design by Amber Stone

Printed in United States of America
IngramSpark Publishing
Publication Date: 2020
ISBN-978-0-578-77245-5

TABLE OF CONTENTS

ACKNOWLEDGEMENTS

It is humbling to me to realize how many hours of computer time and talent that went into this manuscript. Those hours were done by my devoted wife (because I am a caveman and don't touch the computer). Frances has spent literally years learning to use the computer. Then the cover design & polishing touch was from my daughter-in-law, Amber, to whom we are truly grateful. A certain amount of direction & encouragement came from an author friend Dr. Donald M. Minter, Flagstaff AZ. Last but not least for sure, thanks go to the Holy Spirit who certainly hounded my mind with urgency to write most of these titles.

I am grateful for the generous endorsements by my former (retired) Chaplains. It is interesting that my last Chaplain (Col. John South, '94-'95 time frame) endorsed VOL I; then my first Chaplain boss (Col. Curt Bowers, '72-'73 time frame) endorsed VOL II.

INTRODUCTION

It is my desire to have a perspective that avoids the narrow boundaries invented by teams of like-minded theologians. - ("Religion Divides" - Note 32) "Cutting through the chase" is my goal and writing style. If these essays stir up interest in the Bible or Christ, and lead to even one (1) soul finding God, then I will be satisfied. These "Gospel-notes" can be used as free tracts. Just print them out on standard 8 1/2 x 11 printer paper, then fold them two times each way so that the title is on top. The index is link 0 which also prints out on standard paper. Feedback can be put on the Facebook page "Fred J Stone". I was born & raised in South Phoenix, AZ. After graduating high school in '69, I joined the Army to be a helicopter mechanic/door gunner. I served a year in Viet Nam & made a deeper commitment to follow Christ in '72. God confirmed the relationship with many miracles. Then in '77 came a dynamic revelation of Jesus Christ in a spiritual dream ("I Saw the King" - Note 7). And I try to put my miracles & spiritual events into the fabric of the "notes". If those "events" are real, it would be wrong to forget or deny them. Interesting enough, those who call me a liar are usually established religious folk & ministers. (To those critics my only response is, "I am not a crook".)

I spent most of my 21-year Army career as a Chaplain's assistant. During that time, in '73 I married Fran and we had 3 kids (one adopted); and studied for civilian ministry through Berean School of the Bible, Springfield, Missouri. The "gospel-notes" began in about '77 as a natural outflow of military ministry & outreach to soldiers. This writing ministry & additional "notes" have continued for the 40 years since then. Most Scripture refs. are from the Revised Standard Version because that is where I started studying Scripture in '72. Other versions are New American Standard, New International Version, and of course the venerable King James Version. We tend to be non-denominational and are not endorsed by any particular group.

We have restored several homes in Oklahoma & Arizona, then got a contractor's license & built new ones. My wife and I manage & maintain rental property, which we built locally. We attend church in Cottonwood, AZ, both Protestant & occasionally Catholic.

A word about evangelism. "Evangelism is just one beggar telling another where to find bread." D.T. Niles, New York Times, May 11,1986. "For I am not ashamed of the gospel of Christ; it is the power of God for salvation to everyone who has faith, to the Jew first and also to the Greek." Romans 1:16

* * F. J. Stone * *

My website is: www.gospelnotes.net

101

DECISIONS 101

Daily we make decisions on all subjects. What time to rise, what to eat for B. L. or D., what to wear, what's the plan today, which dog to bathe first, should I buy the Ford or the Toyota, which state to call my permanent residence, etc. etc. It appears that life is loaded with decisions, small and large. I believe a decision on the origin of our species is possibly the most subtle and far reaching personal decision, so here it is: Did our ancestors crawl out of the ocean? (Much like a Japanese Mud Skipper – Google it.) -- Or – did our ancestors crawl out of the Garden of Eden after being evicted by God? How we understand the world & man & God & history is muchly affected by one origin decision or the other, when we choose.

If we decide for the Darwin THEORY, then the world has to be hundreds of millions of years old. Our distant "Mud Skippers" became monkeys, then apes, then those wonderful Neanderthals, Cro-Magnons, Piltdown man, Clovis people, etc. (Most of these have been fabrications by eager evolutionists.) Consequently, most of Bible teaching & answers appear to be just silly myths, because basically man created God to fulfill his religious needs. I find the Darwin path to be DECEITFUL because it always was a THEORY but has been force fed to pupils & students from grade 1 to college and beyond. Now we have a nation of intelligent people who are immunized/vaccinated AGAINST faith in God by the subtle theories they were systematically led to believe as FACT. The U.S. and much of the western world has a shrinking Godly value system and are falling into liberal hopelessness. (Lucifer & his demon associates are and always were smooth operators.) Many churches are neglected, and the jails are full . . .

If we decide for the Eden eviction because we failed God, we are acknowledging Him as a basis of thought. We were created by, and accountable to that God of Genesis. We are respecting the Word of God, and it is a progressive revelation of God, man, the world & time, eternity, etc. Fallen man's need of salvation is a constant theme. From the Bible we can learn what FAITH is, and how it activates man's relationship with God if we seek Him. Answers such as – How did B.C. people and Jews find salvation before Jesus came along? – What about all the OTHER religions of the world if Jesus is the only way? – etc. etc. – are available if we are open to Biblical answers. (Many souls are not open to those answers because they are set in the decision of the Mud Skipper Daddy.) For an interesting look at creation & evolution questions, a very good website to check out is www.AnswersInGenesis.org/answers.

Now I love the gospels – how they give the account of Jesus. He dealt with all kinds of people & situations. Ironically, the Jews who had the most education – the Pharisees – were the most difficult for Christ to reach. They had their stubborn traditions of unbelief, so they contradicted Jesus frequently, and accused Him of even being possessed. Ultimately, they had Christ executed. It's the same today. "The god of this world hath blinded the minds of them that believe not, lest the light of the glorious gospel of Christ, who is the image of God, should shine unto them." 2 Corinthians 4:4 But to those who loved & believed in Jesus, he explained everything. (And I think some of them took notes . . .) ". . . privately to his own disciples he explained everything." Mark 4:34b When we walk with Christ as a friend, answers on many subjects just seem to appear. "But the path of the righteous is like the light of dawn, which shines brighter and brighter until full day." Proverbs 4:18

Decisions – I think that's why each person is on this planet. I would encourage all to go with the Eden decision. That is, we came from there, and the Book shows the way to regain "paradise" – God's blessing in this world, and heaven in the next. Choose Jesus, He is Alive, AND He is the way. See also "The Big Lie" note 191.

102

THE STEAM ROLLER

We think of the Steam Roller as a large heavy road machine that flattens the asphalt & leaves it smoking hot. The Book of Isaiah in the middle of the Bible is similar. It has majesty & grandeur, and rolls over questions like “Who made the universe?”, “Who made the earth & owns it?”, “Who has power over death?”, “What about other gods & faiths?”. Isaiah shows the throne of God, man’s accountability to Him, His disdain for astrologers, disdain for human pride, much predictions of Jesus Christ & his 2nd coming, was most quoted by Jesus & the Apostles, AND the resurrected Christ in Revelation. To add “insult to injury” Isaiah is a microcosm of the whole Bible by having 66 chapters. (The Bible has 66 books.) The following clips show something of God’s attitude & frankness.

Starting with the THRONE in Chapter 6:1 “In the year that King Uzziah died I saw the Lord sitting upon a throne, high and lifted up; and his train filled the temple.” That description of God goes on & on and is awesome & the phrase “Lord of Hosts” is used, which is a reference to creation of the universe. “Lord of Hosts” is repeated numerous times in the following 20 or so chapters. Then we have the judgment of the earth in chapter 24 (which parallels Matthew 24 - also dealing with the end of time). It takes a SOVERIGN God to OWN and judge this planet . . . In chapter 25 we see the power to eliminate death & remove all tears. Then in chapters 36 & 37 is a historical reference to God being CHALLENGED by the king of Assyria – Sennacherib & his great army of 185,000 soldiers. This AMAZING incident is also recorded in 2 Kings 18 and 2 Chronicles 32 which suggests the weight of it. (God won the challenge by eliminating the army & the king.) And Isaiah himself was there to witness the event. Chapter 44 shows us that God has no competition, v 6. - “Thus, says the Lord, the King of Israel and his Redeemer, the Lord of hosts: I am the first and I am the last; besides me there is no god.” (Jesus Christ quoted/claimed this after His resurrection - three times.) Moving along to chapter 45:22 we have this, “Turn to me and be saved, all the ends of the earth! For I am God, and there is no other.” (Now according to Scripture, people & nations can have a slick religion, but no god. What a sad picture that is.) Isaiah steam rolls astrologers in chapter 47:13-14. In chapter 53 we have the gospel of Christ 700 years B.C., v.5, - “he was wounded for our transgressions, he was bruised for our iniquities . . .” all of that page is INTENSE. Isaiah/

God steam rolls human pride in chapter 57 v. 15. (And the scope of this essay abbreviates MUCH of the glory of this choice Old Testament book of Scripture.)

Now this God of Isaiah claims to be VERY great, but why is He not self-displayed in this day & age? Too often God seems to be subdued/ hidden & we have to search/seek for Him. The Apostle Paul was encouraged by the resurrected Jesus Christ at night, Acts 23:11. That same Almighty Christ could have promoted/defended himself easily in broad daylight. Maybe we see the humble, kind NATURE of God in His patience. Maybe His overwhelming power & glory & character is gradually revealed to us, to humble us today. Isaiah 45:15 At any rate Isaiah's God is still the LORD of Lords and KING of Kings.

Even though making a stand with Isaiah sometimes leaves our critics "smoking hot", I want to believe in Isaiah's Biblical God because if it's true, it makes ME a King's kid. And God HAS confirmed my faith in Him for over 48 years, which is why I write Gospel-notes. Would YOU like to be a King's kid? Would YOU like to put human pride & ego on the back burner & just go for it? It is possible even though there is opposition inside us AND all around us. But the touch & blessing & destiny of God is worth it, "because, if you confess with your lips that Jesus is Lord and believe in your heart that God raised him from the dead, you will be saved." Romans 10:9 Choose Jesus, He is Alive. See also "What is Saved?" note 39.

103

THE MINDSET OF VICTORY

Is there a mindset of victory? For the scholar, I have been told there is. The "hell bent for election" politician is a classic example of determination to win. For the soldier, I've been told by combat survivors, "we will eat the bugs & rats & snakes, just let us continue to fight." Look at our national football teams & their "do or die" determination on the gridiron. It appears that many arenas of life have a mindset of victory. What about in one's faith arena? Specifically, Biblical faith. This essay looks at elements of Victory - for living & dying well, but let's put the "other side of the coin" first.

Elements of defeat – Probably atheism is high on the defeat list. Darwin & his Atheist's bible "On the Origin of Species" has had a profound impact on the human mind. Biblical creation by God is undermined AND humorous when compared to the theories (accepted as fact) of Darwin. From the theories of evolution, we logically dismiss faith which God requires to reach out to Him and be saved/blessed. Then, of course the Scriptures fall from glory to the level of man's inventions. Then living in any kind of victory is only possible as long as we have human power & youth, and eternal hope is not much of an option. To die is just simply to be done or gone – nothing more. All that commotion from religious folks & the church appears to be a fantasy. Let's just "eat, drink, & be merry for tomorrow we die." Isaiah 22:13 Too many of these folks have the common attitude, "who cares, it doesn't matter, when you are dead, you are just dead." (See note 79 "Rude Surprises".) Other less subtle elements of defeat "are plain – immorality, impurity, licentiousness, idolatry, sorcery, enmity, strife, jealousy, anger, selfishness, . . . drunkenness, carousing, and the like." Galatians 5:19 What a load of negative mindset & defeat.

Elements of Victory – If we are created by God & have a life beyond earth, the faith dimension should be VERY valuable. And there should be some kind of "instruction manual" to explain common questions & issues of faith & life - if God invented life & has integrity Himself. Enter the Scriptures or Word of God (very old stuff here). Whereas the atheists above have created a sophisticated machine & philosophy to bury the Word, the Christian believer holds the Word in high regard. "Forever, O Lord, thy Word is firmly fixed in the heavens. I rejoice at thy Word like one who finds great spoil." Psalm 119:89, 162 KJV And I personally find it amazing that Jesus Christ is mysteriously related to It in His Person. "In the beginning was the Word, and the Word was with God, and the Word was God." John 1:1 (I believe undermining & rejecting the Scriptures has to be a fundamental sin on the level of Blasphemy of the Holy Spirit.) A huge element of Victory is tapping into God's power according to Scripture teaching. Too many people of faith try to "make the grade" on their own power & wits but often stagnate. Another element of V. is the presence. (See note 73 "Divine Presence".) Another excellent element is optimism. Philippians 4:8 sums that up real clearly.

Finally, I would say the "Mindset of Victory" should be more valuable to the Christian than to any other people group, if we live on, beyond the grave – which is a clear teaching of the Book. Below are a few Scripture "mentions" of the Victory – and they define it better than I have.

- Isaiah 40:31 KJV "they that wait upon the Lord shall renew their strength; they shall mount up with wings as eagles; they shall run, and not be weary; and they shall walk and not faint."
- Habakkuk 3:19 KJV "The Lord God is my strength, . . . and he will make me to walk upon mine high places." (The best version of YOU – the Word does teach health, healing, and general wellness.)
- Acts 20:32 "now I commend you to God and to the word of his grace, which is able to build you up and to give you the inheritance among all those who are sanctified."
- Philippians 4:13 KJV "I can do all things through Christ which strengtheneth me."
- 2 Timothy 1:7 KJV "God hath not given us the spirit of fear; but of power, and of love, and of a sound mind."

The above Scripture references amount to "the Mindset of Victory". And I use Scripture because I don't know of a better source of information. If it's true like God claims, then nothing else comes close. I would say to anyone who desires to win, or live in the victory, Choose Jesus and His Word. They are Alive. And be blessed in the Victory. See also "Comfort From Above", note 136.

104

THE LEASE

The landlord/tenant business has been interesting. We started 40 years ago in Lawton Oklahoma. We owned the duplex and the cottage in back, fixed them up real pretty, then made the lease & policy to fit our needs & desires. My Army boss had several units and only made handshake agreements. We wanted a written lease which people agree to and sign. We quickly learned that about 2/3 of them "cut corners" and violate the lease and property. This results in unfair wear & tear, serious property damage, unit down time, litigation, landlord heartburn, etc. Some landlords become DISTRAUGHT with the constant lies, sad stories, animal urinated carpets, false accusations, broken leases, ruined doors, holes in walls, late rent, hot checks, prostitution, blocked communication, and many other troublesome issues. Then with class struggle being what it is, some tenants would kill the landlord if they could – I have personally been hit, soon after beginning my property management career in 1979.

The connection is clear that God is the biggest landlord of this planet, owning the land and all the humans. Psalm 50:10 KJV "For every beast of the forest is mine, and the cattle on a thousand hills." Ezekiel 18:4 "Behold, all souls are mine; the soul of the father as well as the soul of the son is mine: the soul that sins shall die." He has revealed his lease policy to mankind for thousands of years now in the Scripture – indeed the whole Bible can be seen as God's written lease. Interesting enough, in the book of Genesis, maybe two thousand years were on a "hand shake" basis, (which didn't work especially well with the Divine destruction of the antediluvian world of Noah and of course Sodom & Gomorrah at the time of Abraham). Then God presented a concise "written lease" thru Moses in the 10 commandments. Those "thou shalt nots" – idolatry, blasphemy, violating the Lord's day, murder, adultery, lying, etc. And it would appear that God is the most premier DISTRAUGHT landlord these days, judging by the violation of those commandments, and the decline of decent values we see all over the world.

Jesus Christ offered a "lease" story that hits the spot. "A man planted a vineyard, and set a hedge around it, and dug a pit for the wine press, and built a tower, and let it out to tenants. . . When the time came, he sent a servant to the tenants, to get from them some of the fruit of the vineyard. And they took him and beat him and sent him away empty handed." Mark 12:1-9 This story goes on to the killing of the son of the vineyard owner, which presents a clear picture of the Atonement of Christ. - "God so loved the world that he gave his only Son, that whoever believes in him should not perish but have eternal live." John 3:16

Well, in the same sense that people neglect the lease and make a MESS of the landlord's property & mind, people neglect God's lease and make a MESS of their own lives. And God knows He has no perfect tenants. "All have sinned and come short of the glory of God" Romans 3:23 KJV This means we all need Christ's Atonement above to make amends for violating His righteous lease policy. Why not step into a "new lease" today? Jesus paid the "rent" two thousand years ago on the bloody cross.

- Acts 4:12 KJV "There is none other name under heaven given among men, whereby we must be saved."
- 2 Corinthians 6:2b KJV "Behold, now is the accepted time; behold, now is the day of salvation."
- Hebrews 2:3 KJV "How shall we escape, if we neglect so great salvation, which at the first began to be spoken by the Lord and was confirmed unto us by them that heard him."

Choose Jesus, He is Alive. Find a legitimate Bible believing church & support it. God's blessing will be released to you. See also "The Blessing & the Curse" note 66.

105

NEAR-DEATH EXPERIENCE

Much has been said in the last 30-40 years about the near-death experience – NDE. Specifically, it means to actually DIE then come back and tell the story. People have a bad sickness or an accident or total heart failure, then lose consciousness in coma, etc. then go out of body and look on as doctors, medics, nurses etc. frantically try to revive the patient. From this point they usually mention going thru a long tunnel towards a bright light, etc., etc. Great peace and love are mentioned along with meeting long gone family members, angels, a beautiful blissful environment, etc. Then they reluctantly return to their bodies & recover. One PHD Raymond Moody, "Life After Life" 1975 had a lot to say on this subject. I recently read Eben Alexander's "Proof of Heaven" 2012 - and this guy is a brain surgeon.

Doctor Alexander was amazed that his consciousness could leave his dying body. Most medical folks believe the billions of brain cells working together generate what we know as consciousness & soul. They have a problem with the Biblical concept of a soul being independent of the body & mind. And this doctor waxed quite religious in his out of body state. He writes in his chapter 14, "The (false) suspicion that we can somehow be separated from God is the root of every form of anxiety in the universe, and the cure for it . . . was the knowledge that nothing can tear us from God, ever." Really now, does he believe ALL are saved & on their way to glory where Charles Manson & Adolf Hitler will stroll along arm in arm with Billy Graham & Mother Theresa??

Right there is the problem with the stories of NDE's or out of body experiences. These writers are typically NOT theologians but dance all over Divine material & try their best to define it. They go for the gifts of God but deny His revealed character & policies in the Scriptures. Now I appreciate their supposed experiences, as long as they agree with established Bible truth which has been revealed to mankind and recorded since Abraham & Moses, Exodus 24:4. But these "Johnny come lately" amazing stories have a STRONG New Age flavor which can be VERY misleading. People should realize that in this last days world we live in, our adversary & his army of demon spirits have power & are desperate to deceive people on the subject of divine salvation. Specifically the one-way system the Biblical God has established at great cost – blood salvation thru His son Jesus Christ,

John 3:16. New Age and its NDE stories don't recognize the sin problem (or consequences), and suggest we can walk right into heaven as we are.

To be rational on the subject of NDE we should open God's Book and read it. There are frequent accounts of dealing with the living God, along with an out of body experience (1 Samuel 28:11-15), visions of heaven, the SIN problem, God's answer for that, and LOTS of other penetrating truths on various subjects. Why put a lot of stock (and confidence) in a NEW approach? Especially when it almost always contradicts that Old Standard – the Bible. And to BALANCE the NDE supposed pictures of heaven, see Maurice Rawlings "Beyond Death's Door" 1978. This guy was a cardiologist and brought some of his patients back who were falling into hell.

I believe people have a basic DECISION to make. 1) Go for the "of late" answers to ultimate questions & take their chances. - or 2) Go for the ancient & proven path, "Thus says the Lord: Stand by the roads, and look, and ask for the ancient paths, where the good way is and walk in it, and find rest for your souls." Jeremiah 6:16 Paul the Apostle (who had an interesting NDE in Acts 9) said this "I delivered to you as of first importance . . . that Christ died for our sins in accordance with the Scriptures . . ." 1 Corinthians 15:3. Then Jesus (who had a total death experience and came back to discuss it) "I am the way, and the truth, and the life; no one comes to the Father but by me". John 14:6 In over 45 years of study on the subject, I conclude the Old Way is the right way, and the only way that is safe. Choose Jesus, He is Alive. See also "New Age" note 56.

106

HOME OWNERSHIP TECHNIQUE

This "Home Ownership Tech." is a revision of my original 4-page document of 1983. Both the old version and especially this new one can pass as Gospel notes, because they are "good news" to anyone who is tired of paying rent. And I care about the well-being of my readers & want to share a valuable & practical method of owning their own home outright in about 10 years or so. (The original was a system to have the house paid for in 7 years which worked quite well but was more "cave man" & labor intense.)

Most folks expect to pay substantial rent, or even higher mortgage payments to secure decent housing. This H.O.T. offers a practical plan to beat the system. The last 40 years or so have produced lots of motor homes which now are usable but not as pretty. They are also selling at 5% or less of original cost. (We recently bought a 27' MH for $160, which had low miles but fixable rodent damage.) This H.O.T. uses an old motor home (or camp trailer) for 2 years to save rent money. If one can find a cheap place to park the coach, it's much easier to save money. Maybe a friend or relative's back yard? Gypsy style living is not impressive, but it is a necessary part of the plan. Saving a thousand $ or more a month is doable for couples who work. That amount in 2 years is $24,000. More determination equals more saved . . .

Now HUD constantly acquires new listings which are usually re-possessed homes from various sad circumstances of previous buyers. These homes are all sizes, and in all sections of town/city. Some need work, and some are in pretty good shape. They sometimes sell for 70 - 80% of market value to the top bidder. With a 20 – 30K down payment, and a full or 1% over list price, the bidder has a good chance of buying the house. And FHA offers subsidized interest rates. A few tips:

- Know which realtor in your town/city specializes in HUD and get the local/regional details.
- Become pre-qualified w/FHA & HUD so there are minimum delays when you are ready to bid.
- Keep track of all new listings as they are posted frequently.
- The more cash down payment, the lower the monthly payment will be, $500. – 600. a month on a 15-year note is feasible for a nice home. AND paying an extra $200. each month on the principle would shorten the

payoff dramatically. 10 years is also feasible. (Of course, dealing with HUD may not work in all states, due to red tape & lending policies.)

Our personal experience 35 years ago with the H.O.T. involved buying mobile homes & restoring them for resale profit. We did a few, each bigger & more valuable. Then we cashed out of trailers & bought a regular house which was trashed by years of careless tenants. That "caveman" system was very profitable & we never had a regular mortgage. TODAY I'd have a decent $ saved & look for an older house that needed a cosmetic tune-up. And there are property owners that will carry the balance after a decent down. This system will have less red tape & may even offer a better price discount than HUD. This H.O.T. was current in about 2014 – today the numbers above may need to be adjusted for inflation.

So, let's apply the Home Ownership Technique to a higher-level endeavor. Is there a technique to owning a "home" in the sky? Most folks want to have "security" in the next life but how do we attain it? As with a home in this world, a secure and decent place in the "sky" does not come automatically. We need a "technique." I believe God's plan of salvation is the only safe one:

A – ADMIT, "All have sinned and fall short of the glory of God," Romans 3:23

B – BELIEVE, "Believe in the Lord Jesus, and you will be saved," Acts 16:31

C – CONNECT, "Where two or three are gathered in my name, there am I in the midst of them." Matthew 18:20 KJV We should be involved in a Christian church to show God we mean business. See also note 9 "Serving God". Choose Jesus, He is Alive.

107

MESSED UP PICTURES

For a hundred years or so we have had abstract art from such famous names as Picasso, Pollock, and Kandinsky. Instead of the beauty of nature, structure, form & order we see bizarre designs that challenge all the above. But not just in the "field" of art do we find "messed up pictures".

- Trinidad, Colorado where a brilliant surgeon with medical credentials & serious initials after his name, altercates a willing man's genitals into womanhood for a large quantity of money.
- A delusional loner goes into a movie theatre dressed like Bat Man & murders a dozen people with assault weapon. Then the U.S. court system spends millions $ on the case & takes years to decide if he is guilty.
- Suicide airline pilots who take hundreds of innocent folks with them when they die for Allah.
- How about that movement of murderous radical Muslims who believe in a recent (570-632 A.D.) "prophet" rather than the ancient revelations of God which predate Mohammed by thousands of years.
- Then we have a modern politically correct religion where liberal is good and blending all Eastern concepts of God is better. Job 1 is to welcome all faiths except the one that's most reliable & established – Biblical Christianity. See "New Age", note 56.
- The last M.U.P. may be the most cock-eyed. Americans ashamed of their heritage after 250 years of improving the world with order, food production, schools, hospitals, AND saving the world from Nazis, Imperial Japanese, and aggressive Communism.

The above "pictures" point to a "fly in the ointment" of modern life and thought. I believe that fly appeared early – even in the garden. That contradiction of God by our adversary, "Did God say . . ." Genesis 3:1-5, appears to be the ROOT of all "messed up pictures". Since that 1st lie, instead of seeking Biblical beauty, structure, form, and order such as truth & justice, honesty & productivity, our race falls into sin, chaos, & worthless pursuits. Maybe the most insane case of M.U.P was the execution by man of God in the flesh which we see graphically in the final chapters of each gospel – Matthew, Mark, Luke, & John. No wonder the "pictures" of this fallen world can be so "messed up".

- Psalm 37:4 "Take delight in the Lord, and He will give you the desires of your heart."
- Proverbs 13:21 "Misfortune pursues sinners, but prosperity rewards the righteous."
- Isaiah 40:31 KJV "They that wait upon the Lord shall renew their strength; they shall mount up with wings as eagles . . ."
- John 14:23 "If a man loves me, he will keep my word, and my Father will love him, and we will come to him and make our home with him." (J.C.)
- 1 Corinthians 2:9 KJV "But as it is written, Eye hath not seen, nor ear heard, neither have entered into the heart of man, the things which God hath prepared for them that love him."
- 1 Peter 3:12 "The eyes of the Lord are upon the righteous and his ears are open to their prayer."

Please allow me to conclude with one final "messed up picture". A man put bags of money in his attic so he could grab the "dough" on his way up at the time of his demise. But just to be safe, he also put a small Walmart air conditioner in his basement so he could grab it on the way down – he had heard it would be hot in hell, Luke 16:24. Well sadly he died without the salvation of Jesus, and went down with the AC – but to his dismay he couldn't find anywhere to plug it in. (my dry sense of humor there) Choose Jesus, He is Alive. And promote beauty, structure, form & order in your life's "picture". See also "The Blessing and the Curse" note 66.

108

FOUNTAIN OF YOUTH

This is a concept that appeals to aging folks more each year as they see & feel the lack of youthful vigor "slip-sliding away". The Fountain of Youth – F.O.Y. -- is a spring & pool of water that restores the youth of anyone who bathes in or drinks of it. Such legends go back at least 2500 years to one Herodotus "Father of History" a Greek historian. It is said that the Spanish explorer Ponce De Leon was searching for the F.O.Y. when he discovered Florida around 1513. And there is a natural spring in St. Augustine, Florida (oldest U.S. city), which has drawn tourists for over 100 years, folks say it is the F.O.Y. Ponce de Leon discovered.

At any rate, aging is obviously a HUGE problem & people will entertain themselves with myths to be cheered up. Mark Twain with his dry sense of humor later in his life reflected that "Life would be infinitely happier if we could only be born at the age of 80 and gradually approach 18."[1] And how about the billboard ads by plastic surgeons – "Aging is Optional"??[*]

As a student of the Bible I find hints of the Fountain of Youth & healing waters. Isaiah 58:11 KJV "the Lord shall guide thee continually, and satisfy thy soul in drought, and make fat thy bones and thou shalt be like a spring of water, whose waters fail not." Jesus did send a blind man to the "pool of Siloam" for healing of his eyes in John 9:5-7. And even though Jesus did say, "I am the bread of life . . ." John 6:35, "I am the door . . ." John 10:9, "I am the way . . ." John 14:6, "I am the vine . . ." John 15:5. He did not say "I am the Fountain of Youth." But it's obvious that followers of Christ generally live longer with less health compromises like premature aging from hard & stressful living. I recently worked with an 82-year-old Christian auto mechanic who "danced" all around, and under the car we paid him to fix. I could barely keep up even though I'm about 20 years younger. But the Fountain of Youth is supposed to RESTORE youth, not just extend life.

So, is there a real Fountain of Youth? I believe there is, and we find it in that supernatural land called Heaven. In the gospels Jesus spoke much of Heaven, so the existence of the place rests on the integrity of the Scriptures & Christ's integrity – did He tell lies or the truth? And one of the very interesting features of Heaven is a RIVER that starts small flowing from the temple, then expands greatly as it flows toward the east.

Ezekiel 47. This is the real Fountain of Youth. Then this same RIVER is described in the New Testament in Revelation 22:1. It's the "River of water of life, bright as crystal, flowing from the throne of God. . ." Trees & fruit are mentioned both places. Now there are current books written by folks who have had a glimpse of Heaven. One is by a Rebecca Springer who writes of going down into the "river" to experience supernatural water & some of its properties. (Chapter one "Within Heaven's Gates" 1984 acquire thru Amazon.) She also writes of seeing previously departed relatives who were YOUNG in Heaven. I personally had a "glimpse" of my 2-year departed 79 yr. old mother who was YOUNG there (and exuberant with joy & peace). Then "Beyond Death's Door" 1978 by Maurice Rawlings, MD also has powerful glimpses of Heaven. (See also "Near Death Experiences", note 105).

Well, I realize the concept & finding the Fountain of Youth has been a laughing matter for folks. And if Heaven is the place we find it, there is still the problem of having to die to get there. But we all have to die anyway. Why not die with HOPE and a sure promise of seeing Heaven and the Fountain of Youth?? Jesus made it clear for us (and paid the price). "I am the way, the truth, and the life; no man cometh unto the Father, but by me." John 14:6 KJV Choose Jesus, He is Alive. And look forward to swimming in the real "Fountain of Youth". See also "Old Age" note 63.

*"The closest thing (in this world) to the F.O.Y. is physical exercise." Stanton University professor.

109

SEED FAITH

This is a phrase coined by a very successful evangelist from the '50's. Oral Roberts was from the Bible Belt of the U.S. – Oklahoma. He had Methodist roots but went farther with his concept of Christianity into Divine Healing & the Prosperity Doctrine. He wrote "The Miracle of Seed Faith"* in 1976 and many other books. The University bearing his name is a successful conservative Christian school today with nearly 4,000 students in Tulsa, OK. My condensed version of Oral Roberts' "Seed Faith" is this: **God is your source. When you have a NEED, Plant a good SEED. Give God your best, And expect His best. Then pray for the "beast" that is like you the least. Finally, expect a Miracle.** (The part about the "beast" I added, but it fits well.) Seed Faith is a spiritual law that basically says give specifically according to your needs, praying as you go. If you need a job, give labor. If you need friendship, befriend someone. If you need more money, give more to a legitimate cause, etc., etc. Your action will move the hands & resources of God towards you. And the better personal harvest will appear when our giving & praying become systematic & regular. Seed Faith may be close to the "heart & lungs" of a lasting relationship with God BECAUSE:

- we are looking up to God as OUR SOURCE
- we are admitting to God we have needs – the proud usually can't
- it does something SCRIPTURAL about needs
- it promotes giving & prayer which invigorates spirituality
- it deals with common adversity (See Proverbs 16:7)
- it practices expectation
- it believes God supplies needs & does miracles today

These elements get quickly into a personal FAITH relationship which God honors today as He always has.

Now some will hasten to say that S.F. uses God for personal benefit & puts a "selfish" MOTIVE on seeking God. I have been considering the thoughts of a PHD author on the subject of stress relief. This misguided guy writes "Giving is its own reward . . . As you give more freely of yourself . . . you will experience more feelings of peace . . ." He also suggests good deeds without a motive – because after all, humans are righteous by nature. Well, I think humans are NOT righteous by nature (Romans 3:10-11) & we basically need a more earthly MOTIVE – especially for righteous deeds.

And if Jesus Christ himself suggests the personal benefit motive, what is wrong with it?

Jesus said this about Seed Faith, "Give & it will be given to you, good measure, pressed down, shaken together, running over, will be put into your lap. For the measure that you give is the measure you will get back." Luke 6:38 Paul the Apostle put it this way, "He who sows sparingly will also reap sparingly, and he who sows bountifully will also reap bountifully." 2 Corinthians 9:6 Paul also wrote, "My God will supply all your needs according to his riches in Christ." Philippians 4:19

Finally, I'd say "Seed Faith" deals squarely with a most difficult part of being Christian – Giving. This tight guy found early on that good deeds like giving, actually come back & stimulate our relationship with God, & that made "the whole enchilada" easier to swallow. And after accepting Christ as Savior, for anyone Seed Faith really is a key to growing in the Lord. "A generous man will himself be blessed . . ." Solomon, Proverbs 22:9 See also notes 28, 30, 72, and 93. Choose Jesus & His value system, they are Alive. And praying in the name of Jesus is a spiritual law that outshines all.

* Eight million were published, some still available today on Amazon.

110

WHAT'S IN THE AIR?

Air is an interesting substance made up of invisible gasses such as Nitrogen, Oxygen, Argon and Carbon dioside & other trace elements. The Earth has an atmosphere that's about 20 miles thick which is denser at sea level but gets thinner as you go up. Humans have trouble with the air from about 15,000 ft. & higher due to lack of Oxygen. Air is useful for enabling birds and aircraft to fly, also for burning up such things as meteors which would make troublesome craters across the landscape. But what is in the air – especially things we cannot see?

- Moisture is a huge element carried by invisible air. Most weather is due to the way heat & moisture interacts in the air. Fog & clouds are visible, but moisture not usually.
- Fragrance such as perfume, light smoke, road-kill skunk aroma, etc. are not visible. (The skunk is one of God's most powerful creatures – dead 4 days & still <u>strong</u>.)
- Flammable gas such as natural gas, acetylene or propane are invisible & can blow the house apart.
- Radio waves carry all kinds of signals for radio, TV, cell phones, etc. In a typical room there will be dozens or maybe <u>hundreds</u> of different radio frequencies & all sorts of interactions – conversations, texting, still pics, movie, you name it – all invisible.
- Magnetism is an invisible <u>force</u> in the air making the compass needle point north. Birds & insects use it for navigation.
- A scientist or doctor could list more technical and invisible "elements" in the air.

From the above "items" in the air it can be said that our air & atmosphere is not necessarily clean, or neutral. And for decades I have reflected on what spiritual things are in the air. Things like Holy Spirit, Angels, demons, etc. Concerning spiritual concepts in the air, I've been asked in a very nasty way, "How can you believe what you can't see?" But that question is weak to anyone who thinks & considers what natural invisible items can be in the air. If there is a God & spiritual elements, why wouldn't they be in the air? Do us humans have the only ability to put invisible things in the air? Can God not use the air He invented for His own purposes? I have personally experienced angels before any commitments to God, and yes, demons too. See "The Demon" note 43.

I believe people who pursue sin with a passion, or smoke dope attract demons to themselves. It's not just the collective mind of our sinful associates (& youth culture), but unseen elements in the air that can & do home in on people, and when demons come near in power, they don't identify themselves as Satanic – deception & disguise wins more customers. Likewise, those who are considering God & seeking Him attract angels to themselves. And there is a network of Divine laws & principles in the air which can enhance & empower the Christian life if applied. See "Faith" note 75. I didn't invent this kind of thinking – the Scriptures clearly reveal it to those who want to know.

- "And you He made alive, who were dead in trespasses and sins, in which you once walked according to the prince of the power of the air, the spirit who now works in the sons of disobedience." Ephesians 2:1-2
- "For we wrestle not against flesh & blood, but against principalities, against powers, against the rulers of the darkness of this age, against spiritual hosts of wickedness in the heavenly places." Ephesians 6:12
- "The thief (Lucifer & his demon buddies) does not come except to steal, and to kill, and to destroy. I have come that they may have life, and that they may have it more abundantly" – Jesus said that. John 10:10
- "Are they not all ministering spirits sent forth to minister for those who are to attain salvation?" Hebrews 1:14 (referring to angels)

To conclude I would say in this mixed "atmosphere" we should breathe in the name of Jesus & the Holy Spirit & Divine principles. Exhale or "breathe" out the unproductive elements of worldliness that are capable of ruining our eternal souls. Choose Jesus, He is Alive. "Behold, I stand at the door and knock. If anyone hears My voice and opens the door, I will come in to him and eat with him, and he with Me." Revelation 3:20 See also note 27 "The World".

111

THE CON JOB

This is a matter of being sold a "bill of goods" and only ending up with paper if that. It is a gimmick that is "old as the hills" starting probably in the garden where the serpent told Eve "Has God said . . .?" That LIE completely changed the course of human & world history. But in everyday applications we have the Con Job on smaller scales:

- Bait & switch where you are sold an item & end up with something of much less value or nothing at all.
- It's a Con Job when you are in jail long term & someone sends you an elaborate & sophisticated pitch on a kind of bond re-sale which will satisfy the court & get you released for the fee of $4000.
- It's a Con Job when you buy a buildable lot in HI & then learn island thinkers have engineered several layers of red tape BEYOND normal mainland processes to get a building permit.
- It's a Con Job when a vocal minority gets the Supreme Court to re-define marriage in the U.S. making what used to be considered "against nature & perverted", to be O.K. & legal.
- It's a Con Job when entire U.S. states & nations accept the "medical marijuana" lie, that it is good & useful, and not a matter of dissipation. A horse by any other name is still a horse.
- It's a Con Job when our universities have presented Darwinian theories & the Big Bang origin of the universe as fact & not just theories. Then too many liberal seminaries promote such unbelief. And today we have a load of ministers who are not believers of the very Book they profess to teach. See "The Big Lie" note 191

The biggest and most universal CON JOB is in the personal arena where people try to convince God or themselves that their own righteousness w/o Jesus is adequate. The Scriptures are adamant about one-way Jesus salvation, and unless folks find a new book of divine wisdom (which are plenteous but false), the CON JOB is accepting something that God has clearly defined as bogus. This CON JOB amounts to losing one's soul to hell, which is an eternal disaster for the individual.

- "There is a way which seemeth right unto a man, but the end thereof are the ways of death." Proverbs 14:12 KJV

- "Truly, truly, I say to you, he who does not enter the sheepfold by the door but climbs in by another way, that man is a thief and a robber;. . . I am the door: if anyone enters by me, he will be saved, and will go in and out and find pasture." John 10: 1 & 9 Jesus said that.
- "The thief comes only to steal and kill and destroy; I came that they may have life, and have it abundantly." John 10:10
- "Beware lest any man spoil you through philosophy and vain deceit, after the tradition of men . . . and not after Christ." Colossians 2:8 KJV

If you have ever been conned & came up short in a transaction, be sure you are not alone; & you have even God's sympathy; Hebrews 4:15. But when it comes to our faith arena, connecting with the risen Christ & His blessing for time & eternity is the REAL DEAL. Why let the world & it's spirit sell you a counterfeit or empty kind of faith? "My people have committed two evils: they have forsaken me, the fountain of living waters, and hewed out cisterns for themselves, broken cisterns, that can hold no water." Jeremiah 2:13 Jesus clearly echoes this thought in John 7:37-38. Don't be conned -- Choose Jesus, He is Alive.

112

WAXING LIBERAL

These days the word "liberal" is as common as dogs, and maybe needs to be defined. It is the condition of being free of restraint, minimum personal rules & accountability, just a general "free spirit" attitude. Seems like most young people prefer this condition, & today's liberal party does have a lot of the youth culture element on board. In politics liberalism desires to identify with the underdogs of society & their interests. But having unlimited political correctness & over killing issues like clean air, racial inequality, gay rights, legalizing questionable drugs, promoting modicum performance, giving the vote to newcomers & children, and handling the U.S. Constitution recklessly, etc, etc. would seem to be unhealthy for the nation.

There is an incident in the Old Testament where Solomon had been king of Israel & just died. His heir son Rehoboam refused the advice of his father's counselors, and went with the advice of his (young) peers on management style. The kingdom quickly fell apart on that liberal approach. 1 Kings 12. I fear that today's "waxing liberal" will not be healthy for the U.S. either. Jesus Christ gave His opinion 2000 years ago, "a kingdom divided cannot stand". Mark 3:24

Of course, Biblical religion is not especially popular with today's young & left liberal party, but has <u>liberalism itself</u> become the national religion?? It is alarming that our universities, which should be open minded & fair, are together on bashing the Bible & the Christian church. They want to be scientific on all subjects, and "have to see it to believe it" – see "Saying No To God" note 53.

On the individual level, is "waxing liberal" something that leads to personal success & fulfillment? Liberalism promotes self interest (& much tattoos), living for money, pride, arrogant (loose) values, abusive to authority, disloyal to parents, unholy lifestyles, etc. (That list of liberal stuff is my paraphrase from the Apostle Paul's "word" on the last days. 2 Timothy 3:1-2) Success & fulfillment calls for things like self discipline, knowledge, work, money management, & faith. Not a loose connection with the responsible elements of life. And "if we stand for nothing, we can & will fall for anything". Anon. (See "The Con Job" note 111.)

Scripture teaches another kind of "waxing":

- “The fear of the Lord is a fountain of life, that one may avoid the snares of death.” Proverbs 14:27
- “Woe to those who call evil good and good evil, who put darkness for light and light for darkness, who put bitter for sweet and sweet for bitter! Woe to those who are wise in their own eyes, and shrewd in their own sight!” Isaiah 5:20-21
- “But this is the man (woman) to whom I will look, he that is humble and contrite in spirit, and trembles at my word.” Isaiah 66:2b
- “Take my yoke upon you and learn from me; for I am gentle and lowly in heart, and you will find rest for your souls.” Jesus Christ, Matthew 11:29

This world & its value system can & will promote “Waxing Liberal”. Now a blunt definition is given by an Orthodox Rabbi I admire. “Modern liberalism simply means becoming “liberated” from the external authority of God.” (from “America’s Real War” pg 271, Daniel Lapin). Only the outcome of this “rejecting God” (Lapin, pg 273) for the nation & the individual cannot be a good thing according to the Bible & history & conservative thinkers. God’s Word warns us: “The wicked shall be turned into hell, and all the nations that forget God.” Psalm 9:17 KJV “Do you not know that friendship with the world is enmity with God? Therefore whoever wishes to be a friend of the world makes himself an enemy of God.” James 4:4 Those are tough teachings that clearly apply to “Waxing Liberal”. I for one, want to be found “waxing towards God”. Choose Jesus & His value system. They bring fulfillment in time & eternity. See also “The World” note 27.

113

GOD'S HUMBLING MACHINE

This world is a character factory – the Creator promoting good traits in people. Traits such as justice, mercy, & humility. Indeed, Jesus Christ came along 2K years ago, as God in the flesh demonstrating that preferred character – "learn of me; for I am gentle and lowly in heart . . ." Matthew 11:29. With Christ's example we should ALL be humble. But of course, there is the tendency to develop ungodly character traits in our high speed, irrational, & competitive world. Now could it be possible that God has a "Humbling Machine" & godly grief that leads some folks away from standard worldly traits such as pride, ego, & self-focus to higher values & focus? In effect personally seeking us? Here is an incomplete list of humbling "grief pills" that appear to be common:

- Hardships & tragedy can come out of nowhere & track folks down.
- Failed romance & the broken heart is common enough.
- I've noticed a pattern where proud young men seem to have (cute) daughters before sons, which softens their hard hearts.
- Career failures after much preparation can be very humbling.
- Birth defects & disease can often produce Godly orientation & rethinking the purpose of life.
- Your kids can be a "Humbling Machine" as they reject your wholesome family value system & choose "Bohemian" values instead, and other forms of "prodigal stuff". . .
- Old age fading can be a "grief pill". I've seen some of the proudest "blokes" become humble (and open to the Gospel) as they get closer to the "pearly gates" & personal judgment.

The premise of this essay is that God can personally pursue & persuade people to go His way. But if we have free will, why would He do that?? I believe those family members (& friends) who are "on the fence" but are actively prayed for by caring mother, father, sister, brother, etc. may have God's attention & life changing "pressures" from Above. Folks who have no one praying for them & have decided against God may well suffer "Strong Delusion" from Above (note 173) and lose their souls. Now Scripture reveals that "it is not God's will that any should perish" 2 Peter 3:9. With God's fore-knowledge of who will choose His program, and who will not, "God's Humbling Machine" may be just His way of hurrying up the process. (This Gospel-note theme dances around the doctrine of Election.) Here's a few Bible refs. that seem to apply:

- Micah 6:8 KJV "He has showed you, O man, what is good; and what does the Lord require of you but to do justice, and to love kindness, and to walk humbly with your God?"
- Proverbs 16:5 KJV "Everyone that is proud in heart is an abomination to the Lord; though hand join in hand, he shall not be unpunished."
- Isaiah 2:12 "For the Lord of hosts has a day against all that is proud and lofty, against all that is lifted up and high;" (I realize the "Day of the Lord" is generally thought to be God's grand scale judgment of earth & humanity at the end of time. But on the small scale of the individual it can also apply.)
- Isaiah 45:7 KJV "I form light and create darkness, I make weal and create woe, I am the Lord, who do all these things."
- 2 Corinthians 7:10 "For godly grief produces a repentance that leads to salvation and brings no regret, but worldly grief produces death."

A current Bible scholar gives perspective on "God's Humbling Machine" – "People don't change because they see the light. They change because they <u>feel the heat</u>." Rick Warren. Well, the main thing is CHANGE. And God cares enough about us to apply personal pressure. See also "Divine Appointments", note 151. Choose Jesus, He is Alive, and become acquainted with an awesome God.

114

STRANGE WORDS

I find words too interesting. They contain lots of facts, which make up our world. If I had to choose only one book (besides the Bible) & go live like Robinson Crusoe on a deserted island, it would be a dictionary. But some words can be strange & confusing:

- burden - refrain of a song
- panic – a kind of grass
- defile – a narrow ravine
- patch – a fool or clown
- surfeit – a nest of skunks
- murder – a line of crows on a fence
- unkindness – a group of ravens
- congregation – a group of alligators

Now internet word lists using "congregation" for alligators seems to be recent since the Oxford dictionary calls a bunch of alligators a BASK. Webster doesn't specify either. I suspect using "congregation" for alligators is derogatory of the Church. But what else is new in our modern world? The church – especially the protestant & catholic groups have lost much luster in the last 50 years or so. The decision to remove prayer from schools & religious plaques from court rooms has had negative trends in our society & world. Separation of church & state doesn't mean evict God or His value system, but that appears to be what we have done.

Regeneration is also a strange word for most people. In biology, the lobster grows a new claw. For humans it means to be spiritually reborn, renewed or restored. This means we <u>need</u> this to be <u>right</u> or <u>whole</u> (exactly what Scripture teaches.) However, today's liberal climate is insulted by such a need being suggested by an Old Book that has been undermined, intellectually by <u>even</u> the church that claims to own it. (See Higher Criticism.) Now regeneration is another word for salvation, which is also a "strange word" today. Lots of folks today have the mindset that says, "I'm OK, and you're OK," don't need no salvation, shut up & sit down . . .

Today the words <u>Regeneration</u> & <u>Salvation</u> are strange to people BECAUSE it's politically correct to <u>never</u> find fault with anyone, on ANY subject. Dale Carnegie's 50's slant on friendship may match today's liberalism – "If you want to keep friends & have people like you . . . never <u>complain</u>, never <u>criticize</u>, and never <u>condemn</u>." (So it was in Christ's day also - He was executed along with most or ALL of the Apostles later on for violating that principle. See John 8:44) Another main reason WHY those words Regeneration & Salvation are strange is because people don't understand God's Ways. He has always done things to amaze & challenge the mind of man. Consider hard core Old Testament miracles, or the Incarnation & Resurrection of Christ.

Another "strange word" is God's definition of salvation: man is lost, Christ dies for our sin, we believe it & are saved, or reject it & remain lost. Man could not & would not invent that Biblical model. The mind of man would cook up something that strokes us (See "New Age" note 56), not a rebuke for sin. It's just God's Way to present such a "strange word" salvation model to humanity. We are being challenged by our creator to see who will "dance" with Him, and who will not. Consider God's Ways in the following:

- "And the Lord God formed man of the dust of the ground and breathed into his nostrils the breath of life; and man became a living soul." Genesis 2:7 (Humble beginning there for our race – dust is pretty cheap.)
- "For my thoughts are not your thoughts, neither are your ways my ways, saith the Lord." Isaiah 55:8
- "For as Jonah was three days and three nights in the wale's belly; so shall the Son of man be three days and three nights in the heart of the earth." Matthew 12:40 Jesus said that.
- ". . .for what is exalted among men is an abomination in the sight of God." Luke 16:15b
- "if anyone is in Christ, he is a new creation; the old has passed away, behold, the new has come." 2 Corinthians 5:17
- "Being born again, not of corruptible seed, but of incorruptible, by the word of God, which liveth and abideth forever." 1 Peter 1:23 KJV I personally believe this passage is a subtle reference to Christ.

Now the written "Word of God" gives us the knowledge of His Regeneration & Salvation (along with a HUGE quantity of other info.) Yes, Regeneration & Salvation may be "strange words" to this world, but valid for thousands of years. Have YOU connected? If not, why not?? "Behold, I stand at the door and knock; if anyone hears my voice and opens the door, I will come in to him and eat with him, and he with me." Revelation 3:20 Choose Jesus and His Word. They are Alive. And serious seekers of Christ should participate in a Bible fellowship – God's people are not alligators, & hardly ever bite.

115

THE PHOENIX BIRD

Being from Phoenix, AZ myself makes the Phoenix Bird myth special. I've seen the "fire bird" symbol on police cars & city buildings etc. as far back as I can remember. But the legend of this famous bird goes back 5000 plus years! Chinese, Egyptian, Arabian, Native American, and others have records of ancient Phoenix bird myths & legends. This bird was rare & long lived - 500 years, with only one living at a time. As large as an eagle, it lived on dew, killing nothing. The Chinese myth included character elements of high virtue & grace, power & prosperity, but a peaceful creature. It was considered the king of birds. Towards the end of its life, the Phoenix bird would build a pyre nest of aromatic branches & spices, then set it on fire with himself in it. Some legends indicate a rebirth of the Phoenix as it rose from the ashes & midst of the flames. This info is basically from the internet.

Now for decades I have thought of myself as a kind of "Phoenix Bird," especially the part of rising again from the ashes & flames. But recently it's become clear that the REAL Phoenix Bird is a character I met over 25 years ago, Police & U.S. Army Chaplain John South. This man had serious challenges from age 7 or so from an abusive stepfather. He joined the Army in '66 to be in the infantry, then got seriously shot in Viet Nam. After discharge became a police officer & dealt with suicide weekly. Sadly, John lost that tough career to war injury health issues. He then entered intense clergy study to become a Chaplain. He rose from the ashes & flames of serious challenges to shine better each time. John humbly gives the credit to his faith in Christ – the essence of HOPE. Dr. John J. South recently published his 163 page excellent book on the subject of Depression, despondency, & suicide – "A Journey Through PTSD".[2] See also "The Chaplains" note 70.

Well, it's not my purpose to shine a spotlight on my old friend (& boss) Col. John South. Actually, I'm using his success story as an example of what God can do when we are down & out. A 50's era Christian hymn had these lyrics "It is no secret what God can do . . ." THAT is the appeal of this Gospel-note essay. When we get to the end of our rope & strength in the "valley of the shadow of death," we can hear His voice and look up. With His touch & Divine Guidance, & REGENERATION, Christ brings us into the best version of ourselves. The hymn above continues to say, "What He's done for others, He'll do for you."[3]

- Isaiah 40:31 "but they who wait for the Lord shall renew their strength, they shall mount up with wings like eagles, they shall run and not be weary, they shall walk and not faint." (The eagle compares to the Phoenix bird.)
- Habakkuk 3:19 "God, the Lord, is my strength; he makes my feet like hinds feet, he makes me tread upon my high places." (The best version of YOU.)
- John 1:12 "But to all who received him, who believed in his name, he gave power to become children of God;"
- Romans 8:28 "We know that in everything God works for good with those who love him, who are called according to his purpose."
- Philippians 4:13 "I can do all things in him (Christ) who strengthens me."

This old world is tough & most honest souls will admit they have "burned" feathers. But there is HOPE in Jesus Christ. The Phoenix Bird myth can find personal application in anyone's life if we only receive Christ & draw on His strength & power. It is then we can begin to realize more of those virtues above – grace, power, prosperity, & peaceful spirit. Choose Jesus, He is Alive. See also "The Eagle" note 50.

116

LAST MIRACLES

Most folks have heard of the miracles of Jesus Christ – walking on water, healing sick, replacing blind eyes, raising dead Lazarus, etc. But the last day or so of his life offers some very unusual miracles, and not as well known:

- Christ predicted that Peter would deny Him 3 times BEFORE the rooster crowed. That happened, Luke 22:34, but only the power of God could stop the rooster from crowing in the morning (unless it was dead).
- When Christ was arrested there was a scuffle & the servant of the high priest got his right ear cut off. Jesus put it back on, Luke 22:50-51.
- There was darkness over the land in mid-day <u>for three hours</u> while Christ was on the cross, Matthew 27:45. If that was only an eclipse of the sun, the timing itself was a serious miracle. (But solar eclipses last 7 and a half minutes or less which means 3 hrs. was a <u>serious</u> miracle.)
- The thick temple curtain ripped in two from top to bottom and earthquake "and the rocks were split". Matthew 27:51 -- that was God's way of saying we now have a New Covenant and direct access to God without a priest. Jesus is our priest, Hebrews 9:11-12, 15. Now a lot of good Christians enjoy a style of Church that has been "priestly" for 1500 years. But those who "protest" can have a <u>fine</u> relationship with Christ directly, 1 Timothy 2:5.
- When Jesus died – "tombs also were opened, and <u>many bodies</u> of the saints . . . were raised, and coming out . . . after his resurrection . . . and appeared to many," Matthew 27:52-53. That Easter morning was much more intense than just Christ coming back to life – there was a whole gang of "resurrectees" milling around Jerusalem.

The "last miracles" of Christ are unique & special and have their own meaning. Anyone who thinks (and believes) can benefit and gain Biblical perspective & FAITH from them. They also get a glimpse of God's character from them. I have personally experienced many miracles (see note 33 "My Miracles"). Now this doesn't mean I'm especially holy or righteous – I have just been open to miracles from the beginning of my Christian experience. And possibly I'm spoiled by miracles. Recently I got my "last miracle" – (hopefully not the final one . . .) We were camping at a forest lake in AZ & I kicked a grapefruit size rock which was cracked. It broke in 2 or 3 pieces. I picked up a fist size piece & looked at the inside fissure surface. To my amazement, there was a wallet photo size image of my 9 yr old granddaughter – a little blurry, but not vague or abstract. We keep it on our breakfast table as a reminder of God's character & power & miracles.

I suppose this "note" can be concluded by simply saying God can do anything, and He is a cool character. If you are looking for inspiration & HOPE, just read & reflect on what miracles have already been done – from "cover to cover," not just the "last miracles" above. The Bible is the book of miracles. And know that, "Jesus Christ is the same yesterday, and today, and forever." Hebrews 13:8 It's comforting to know that miracles still happen, according to our faith & our needs. Of course, with or without miracles, the new birth in Christ is itself a miracle in this ungodly world. "If anyone is in Christ, he is a new creation; the old has passed away, behold, the new has come." 2 Corinthians 5:17 Choose Jesus, He is Alive. (And I know it's not politically correct these days to believe the Bible or it's mysterious miracles, but I sure am enchanted with my new/old Rachel Rock.)

117

THE AGENDA

The word "agenda" is a simple one. Even in a big dictionary it is defined only as a list of things to be done - or - a list of things to be discussed at a business meeting. Then we have the devious "hidden or secret agenda." Commonly we think of an agenda as someone's main purpose. Some of these may be familiar:

- the dog catcher – catch & haul in stray dogs, and maybe an occasional cat.
- the teenage idol – charm the 10-17 year-old with acting or musical talent & rake in as much $ as possible. (But their agenda typically backfires – look at them in 10-20 years . . .)
- the drug addict – get more drugs hook or crook.
- ISIS – kill as many Christians & infidels as possible & let Allah sort them out.
- the EPA, unions, & government agencies – kill small business with red tape, endless petty rules, & regulations.
- the U.S. secular university – educate young people, but make sure their faith is destroyed – especially Christian faith & Biblical concepts.
- human nature – the standard agenda of pride & ego, or "my way or highway" is common enough. See "Human Nature" note 182.

Does God have an "agenda"? According to the Bible, yes there is a Divine Agenda. First, we see creation of the earth & life. Next, we see God revealing Himself. The Book of Exodus & Moses is where that revealing gets very technical & interesting. Page after page it says "The Lord said to Moses" – at least 13 chapters start this way. And Moses was an educated man who WROTE IT ALL DOWN. Exodus 24:4; (But God wrote some of it – the Ten Commandments on stone – Exodus 20.) Next, we see God visiting his creation as a man – Jesus Christ. Next, we see the crucifixion of Jesus Christ as atonement for man's fallen nature & sin. Finally, we see the GOSPEL message intellectualized by Paul, the "grafted in" Apostle, & dramatic example of the new birth. (Acts 9:1-30) Paul wrote much of the New Testament.

There is the overall "agenda" of God. It can be put in a nutshell by these references:

- “For the Son of man came to seek and to save the lost.” Luke 19:10
- “And as Moses lifted up the serpent in the wilderness, so must the Son of man be lifted up, that whoever believes in him may have eternal life.” John 3:14-15
- “And he made from one every nation of men to live on all the face of the earth, having determined allotted periods and the boundaries of their habitation, that they should seek God, in the hope that they might feel after him and find him. . . ” Acts 17:26-27
- “And without faith it is impossible to please him. For whoever would draw near to God must believe that he exists and that <u>he rewards those</u> who seek him.” Hebrews 11:6

I believe those “rewards” just above amount to a Divine Blessing on the seeker’s life, then heaven when we “kick the bucket.” And <u>God’s agenda</u> is not hidden or secret – it is VERY well known. If the individual (you) wants to know, it’s available & basically free information. Sure, some religious groups have tampered with the GOSPEL message, but that hasn’t killed it – Jesus & His salvation is still alive & well, “in spite of hell. Have YOU connected w/God’s agenda?? “Behold, I stand at the door and knock; if anyone hears my voice and opens the door, I will come in to him and eat with him, and he with me.” Revelation 3:20 Choose Jesus & God’s agenda, they are Alive. If we find a Bible believing church & support it, we are showing commitment to “God’s agenda.” See also “What’s In It For Me” note 28.

118

THE CULT PROBLEM

Our modern world has been plagued by the cult problem for decades. Thanks to the family oriented nature of humans, & our need to "fit in". This need for association has produced good things of course, but the cult appears not to be. Then this problem expands into politics & philosophy - Confucianism, Mohammed-ism, Marxism, Socialism, (Cannabis-ism - if this is a cult, I suspect Lucifer himself is the leader of it.) To be American basically means more personal freedom, but the cult drastically reduces that freedom. I believe tender lonely hearted souls often don't know how to resist & say no to the cult's appeals & then don't know how to break away. They get hooked on the smooth talk & VOICE & persona of an apparent leader & follow, but too often there is no place to go . . . There is something to be learned from lemmings. Common religious cults are Mormon, Watchtower, Christian Scientists, Moonies & others. Typically a cult is the thinking of one person, but unfortunately these "organisms" grow, become deep rooted, & live for centuries.

One of the main reasons we are all here is to THINK & sort out the messes & choices of life. And obvious falseness in religion gives ALL faiths a "black eye". Cults start by misrepresenting the nature of God - Father, Son, & Holy Spirit balance is off, or completely altered by going with a totally false god. The creeds of the early church were produced by councils only a couple hundred years after Christ because "cock eyed" doctrines & thought were taking hold even then. Those creeds; Apostolic & Nicene, (340 - 400 A.D.) targeted false doctrine by simply affirming the true Biblical positions. Not many could afford a personal copy of the Bible before the printing press in 1450, so it was much harder then, to "study to shew thyself approved unto God . . . rightly dividing the word of truth." 2 Timothy 2:15 KJV Today we have abundant cheap Bibles & people are mostly literate, AND we still have the simple creeds. There is not much excuse for falling into a cult.

Now some might accuse "Gospel-notes" of just being another cult. Not so - I point folks to Christ & His Word the Scripture, then His Church. And the Word is very complete in exposing false thought in Christianity. The problem today is the Word has been hammered by liberal thought & villainized by "so called" intellectuals. But it still is what it always was - the revealed mind of Christ. We can TRUST it to illuminate our way:

- "Thy word is a lamp to my feet and a light to my path." Psalms 119:105
- "There is a way which seems right to a man, but its end is the way to death." Proverbs 14:12 Cults can & have killed a lot of people.
- Jesus said, "I am the way, and the truth, and the life; no one comes to the Father, but by me." John 14:6
- ❖ "If you confess with your lips that Jesus is Lord and believe in your heart that God raised him from the dead, you will be saved." Romans 10:9 (This ref. & the one below are likely <u>the roots of the creeds above</u>, according to some theologians.)
- ❖ "Therefore, I want you to understand that no one speaking by the Spirit of God ever says "Jesus be cursed!" and no one can say "Jesus is Lord" except by the Holy Spirit." 1 Corinthians 12:3
- "Beware lest any man spoil you through philosophy and vain deceit, after the tradition of men, after the rudiments of the world, and not after Christ." Colossians 2:8

To conclude, if the social element of a group is too strong, be careful that it's not a cult with nothing to offer the individual but a diversion from the proven path, which is Jesus Christ. An old theologian named D.C. Hodge said this, "No road to perdition has ever been more thronged than that of false doctrine. Error is a shield over the conscience, and a bandage over the eyes." Standard Christian churches have something REAL to offer or give. Cults have been known to just TAKE . . . don't get taken. Choose Jesus & His Word, they are Alive. Also see "Imposters" note 57.

119

MEAT IN THE SOUP

This Gospel-note series is kind of like a soup, I think. Various ingredients & flavors all simmering together putting off an aroma. (Some may not like the "fragrance" - see 2 Corinthians 2:15-16), to others it just needs a little "meat" for a better aroma & nourishment. So maybe some basic doctrines should be touched. Like Expiation, justification, regeneration, grace, redemption, etc. The following definitions are from a current Bible Dictionary and Grudem's "Systematic Theology". And as M.F. Unger says, "To believe these things is to enter into the benefits of them."

- Expiation – denotes the end accomplished by certain divinely appointed sacrifices in respect to freeing the sinner from the punishment of his sins . . . preeminently, the offerings which Christ made of himself for the sins of the world. Similar to Atonement. (Unger's Bible Dictionary, 1973 M.F. Unger pg. 335)
- Regeneration – the spiritual change wrought in a person by the Holy Spirit, by which they become the possessor of a new life. A being born again – a change in our moral and spiritual nature.
- Justification – a divine act whereby an infinitely Holy God judicially declares a believing sinner to be righteous and acceptable before Him because Christ has borne the sinner's sin on the cross. 1 Corinthians 1:30; Romans 3:24.
- Grace – there is a common grace for all humans, it's just good stuff like food, water, health, etc. that are not religious items. Saving grace is what God gives believers as per above E., J., & R.
- Redemption – spiritual deliverance from the bondage of sin. Its meaning centers in the atoning work of Christ as the price paid for human redemption, which is why Christ is called the Redeemer.
- Imputation – we know God is righteous but there is also a righteousness which flows from God. Since no human in God's eyes is righteous, Romans 3:10, it is clear that an imputed righteousness is sinful man's only hope of acceptance with a Holy God.
- Gospel – the good news of the death, burial and resurrection of Christ as provided by Him, and preached by His disciples (1 Corinthians 15:1-4). The gospel is full and free deliverance from sin on the basis of simple repentance & faith in Jesus Christ.

- Sanctification – the process of growing in godliness – improvement in our character and conduct by the power of the Holy Spirit within. Separation from the secular & sinful and setting apart for a holy lifestyle.
- Glorification – the transformation of a redeemed person at their life's end. The soul leaves the worn-out shell of the earthly body to enter into the new dimension of God's spiritual kingdom. See 1 Corinthians 15:42-44 ". . . It is sown in weakness; it is raised in power. . ."

Now lots of folks appreciate a religious "veneer" in their life but are hazy as to what elements are in the "soup". And if we don't care/believe in those elements, how can we think they apply to us? We should care due to the eternal importance of our souls. And lots of religious "soups" lack the above "protein rich" elements that stay with the individual through the "heat of the day" (their last judgment by God the inventor of the "meat" elements above). It's "a sad day in Cornville" when "pea soup" religion fails the individual at the most important spiritual event of life – that solemn day of personal reckoning. "On that day many will say to me, 'Lord, Lord, did we not prophesy in your name, and cast out demons in your name, and do many mighty works in your name? And then will I declare to them, 'I never knew you; depart from me, you evildoers.'" Matthew 7:22-23 People who cultivate a healthy & Biblical experience with God don't have to worry about that personal disaster. Choose Jesus, He is Alive. Find a church that teaches & clearly explains the above concepts. See also "What's In It For Me?" note 28.

120

THE NEW AMERICA*

Most people are familiar with the "Old America" - a place of freedom, justice, opportunity, individualism, national pride, honest politics, etc. Many old patriotic & religious songs were born - "This Land is Your Land", "America the Beautiful", "God Bless America". Don't hear those anymore it seems. Now we have people who take this land for granted & seem to focus only on its faults. We even have a president (no. 44) who never was personally inconvenienced with military service to fight for freedom or its principles, but goes around the world apologizing for the U.S. influence for freedom, peace & order (which cost us hundreds of thousands of servicemen's lives in our bloody wars since 1776). Well, now we have a "New America" with the below listed features of "change".

- disregard for those founding principles & even the constitution.
- national decline & major federal debt from reckless waste of tax dollars.
- giving our national Judeo/Christian faith second class standing & putting any "other" faith on better standing. Then atheism is university approved.
- legalized street drugs which produce precious little benefit to society. ("Medical marijuana" is a 93% false argument.) See Isaiah 5:20-21
- a Supreme Court that no longer has the courage to define right & wrong but signs off on popular opinion - even if not the majority popular opinion.
- homosexual marriage is now as legal & govt. approved as the natural style invented & blessed by God.
- government rules & regulations & political correctness nearly to the point of Nazi Germany.
- real estate values very unstable - some down like a lead balloon.
- how about putting combat boots on liberated young ladies? (I can't think of a better way to weaken line units - unless it was to verify gay soldiers which we have also done...)

Well, "change" can be a good & useful thing unless it is moving in the wrong direction. How about changing the baby with a diaper WORSE than the first one? And when we quit time & reason honored traditions of truth, industry, moral & religious integrity, family & economic integrity, etc., we have gone in that wrong direction. I think we are past "love it or leave it" – now it's "love it or lose it", which is exactly what the secular progressive folks are setting us up for. Thanks Obama. . . I would like to believe our America is too secure or holy to collapse, but reason doesn't support that hope. Scripture says this about a nation (or individual's) health & security:

- Proverbs 14:34 "Righteousness exalts a nation, but sin is a reproach to any people."
- Jeremiah 2:11 "Has a nation changed its gods, even though they are no gods? But my people have changed their glory for that which does not profit."
- Psalms 33:12 "Blessed is the nation whose God is the Lord, the people whom he has chosen as his heritage!" (see Deuteronomy 28 for a sobering word on God's Blessing & Curse.)
- 2 Chronicles 7:14 "if my people who are called by my name humble themselves, and pray and seek my face, and turn from their wicked ways, then I will hear from heaven, and will forgive their sin and heal their land."

I really don't like to write negative essays, but the New America from a Biblical point of view is not a positive or a new thing – apostasy, decadence, & decline have been around a long time. But hopefully we can get back on the right track. It is a Biblical principal that "change" has to start with the individual. Have YOU looked up for God's regenerating touch? This is Christ's message of hope for "whosoever will." Jesus said, "If a man (or woman) loves me, he will keep my word, and my Father will love him, and we will come to him and make our home with him." John 14:23 That is the kind of fundamental "change" we need to restore hope on the small scale & the large. And if the "New America" crashes & burns, the saved individual (you) will come out fine in the end. Choose Jesus, He is Alive. Promote God's blessing on your life and be a part of the solution towards healing this nation.

*This G-NOTE was written about 2015.

121

BAD LUCK PILLS

It seems like there are pills for everything these days. Vitamins, prescription drug pills for anything & everything, buzz pills, headache pills, dizziness pills, even cyanide pills for spies when they get caught (?). Some folks have as many as 15 or 20 various drug pills going. My mother had about 7 & lived to 79. My father was pill shy & wouldn't take ANY – he lived to be 85. Maybe too many pills are not good?

Could there be bad luck pills? As in take the "pill" then have bad luck? I believe SIN is a bad luck pill. Especially that pesky besetting sin. It's the one many folks have hanging on them. Maybe it's profanity, lying, stealing, tobacco, alcohol, illegal drugs, gambling, promiscuity, etc. Each soul knows what their besetting sin is because their conscience AND common sense has told them. And according to Scripture, God disciplines people – especially his own redeemed – "judgment starts in the household of God". 1 Peter 4:17

During the conquest of Canaan in the time of Joshua, a character named Achan stole some gold & silver which were "devoted to the treasury of the Lord" by God's command. Achan's "B.L.P." fouled the blessing on Israel's mission & got many killed including himself and his family. (Very interesting Bible account – Joshua chapter 7), of course that was the age of LAW – now we are in the age of Grace, but we are dealing with the same God.

My personal experience with "Bad Luck Pills" for decades is every time I fell to the besetting sin, usually the same day there was bad luck & guilt. And oh how crafty the human mind is in rationalizing sin to be O. K. Then if you (or I) the indulger in a certain type of sin have been enlightened by God or your conscience that it was/is offensive to God, it still will be even decades later – God rarely if ever changes His mind (immutability is a Divine attribute.) Then Jesus Christ said, ". . . sin no more, lest a worse thing come unto thee." (John 15:4 KJV) Is Christ making a point there that more sin equals more bad luck?

Bad luck pills in the unbeliever's life keeps them "unlucky" and unlikely to move towards God. Those "pills" in the believer's life keeps us "unlucky" & damages our relationship with God. It is an awesome feeling to experience undeniable answered prayer & miracles even, but "Bad Luck

Pills" block anything good coming down on us from above. "Beloved, if our hearts do not condemn us, we have confidence before God; and we receive from him whatever we ask, because we keep his commandments and do what pleases him." 1 John 3:21-22 But in the guilt of SIN and hypocrisy we pray less, and we get less. Below are some references that seem to apply:

- Hosea 7:2 ". . . the thief breaks in, and the bandits raid without. But they do not consider that I remember all their evil works. Now their deeds encompass them, they are before my face."
- Proverbs 3:11-12 ". . . do not despise the Lord's discipline or be weary of his reproof, for the Lord reproves him whom he loves . . ."
- Proverbs 28:13 "He who conceals his transgressions will not prosper, but he who confesses and forsakes them will obtain mercy."
- Galatians 6:7 "Do not be deceived; God is not mocked, for whatever a man sows, that he will also reap."
- Hebrews 12:1 "since we are surrounded by so great a cloud of witnesses, let us also lay aside every weight, and sin which clings so closely, and let us run with perseverance the race that is set before us."

So, what is the point of this "Bad Luck Pills" essay? I believe the purpose of life is to find salvation in Christ & be blessed. But "Bad Luck Pills" put a "fly in the ointment" of our very purpose of living. I suppose we should look at those besetting sins and plead the blood of Jesus over them. Only that power can set us free to enjoy "better luck," and/or God's blessing. Choose Jesus, He is Alive. See also "The Blessing & The Curse" note 66.

122

BED BUGS*

It's common knowledge that a good night's sleep is so refreshing & peaceful. And our beds should be a special & clean place to "rest in peace". BUT it seems that these tiny insects can rob folks of sleep. And when we realize the bites and rash on our skin is due to hungry bugs eating us at night, some folks are rattled. In fact, some hotel/motel authorities say bed bugs are a serious national problem even in top-notch establishments.

Well, what about the final establishment we are all headed for – the "city of the horizontal" or "the last motel"? Many of the head stones clearly say, "rest in peace," or "R.I.P.". Are all of those souls really resting in peace, with nothing eating them? Or is there such a thing as bed bugs in eternity? Is the typical cemetery not really as peaceful a place as most folks wish to believe?? Does the liberal notion, "when you're dead, you're problems are over," hold any truth? Does the Bible shed any light on this?

There is an interesting reference to the darker afterlife spoken by Christ Himself in Mark 9:48 "where their worm does not die, and the fire is not quenched." Also Luke 16:24 mentions something less than peaceful sleep in that dreaded "last motel." "Father Abraham, have mercy upon me . . . for I am in anguish in this flame." I'm thinking the bed bugs of this life are a lot more likable than the worms & flames of the afterlife Christ mentioned above. And throughout the Book the doctrine of hell is consistent:

- Psalms 9:17 "The wicked shall depart to Sheol, all the nations that forget God." (For God's definition of "wicked," go to Malachi 3:18, that's the last page of the Old Testament. My definition and yours may not count for much. . .)
- Matthew 13:41-42 "The Son of man will send his angels, and they will gather out of his kingdom all causes of sin and all evildoers, and throw them into the furnace of fire; there men will weep and gnash their teeth."
- Revelation 20:15 "and if anyone's name was not found written in the book of life, he was thrown into the lake of fire."

For a professional "word" on the subject of hell consider reading "Beyond Death's Door" 1978 by Dr. Maurice Rawlings. This guy was a cardiologist, and an original teacher of CPR. He wrote that book because some of his near death patients came back via CPR begging him to save them from the literal hell they had briefly experienced. His super-interesting book can be acquired thru Amazon.

Now of course today it is often <u>NOT politically correct</u> to believe there is a hell to shun or that God is any kind of harsh in judgment, if He exists at all. . . And people accumulate false notions on the subject of eternity without comparing them with the best standard on the subject – the Bible. What a shame when those folks have "rude surprises" and "bed bugs" too late. (see also note 79)

I totally believe all folks should do some homework to challenge their assumptions on the afterlife. A quality study Bible can often be had for about $2 at a thrift store. Of course, a Bible believing church will explain the case also. Gospel-notes should be last on anyone's source list for eternal guidance & study, but they can be helpful too – especially notes 43, 74, 86, & 105. <u>Choose Jesus and his Word, they are Alive.</u> And R.I.P. without "bed bugs" when it's your time to go. . . Christian believers also get blessed while they live.

* This is my Tim Burton style "Gospel-note".

123

TYPES OF POWER

It's amazing how many types of power are out there. From the beginning of time man has discovered:

- Muscle power - the body has 640 muscles which work together to give the human power to walk, run and work.
- Mind power - "work smarter not harder" they say.
- Animal power - plowing with an ox was a better proposition than pick & shovel.
- The power of the flame - it didn't take long for early man to learn that cooked meat tastes better. . .
- Steam power - when James Watt in 1781 patented the steam engine, ships and locomotives entered a new era.
- Wind power - tornadoes & hurricanes are destructive, but the windmill enabled man to gain mechanical advantage from the wind.
- Pneumatic & hydraulic power - the modern world would be paralyzed without P. & H. power.
- The power from oil & gasoline - how many cars, trucks, trains, ships, and aircraft are powered by oil & gas?
- Electricity is a magic kind of power - understood by few but used by all. . .
- The power of the atom - fine & good unless we vaporize half the earth & three quarters of its population by a nuclear war.

The power of God - this type of power is in a totally different (and higher) category. Many today prefer to focus on the sum-total of the above 10 power types and leave God out. Yes, we live in a secular age. A couple of hundred years ago God was more a part of the power picture. Are we wiser now that God is a second-class citizen & most people are blind to His power?

The power of God is revealed and explained in the Bible from cover to cover. We see the early events & development & key characters like Abraham, Moses, David, Isaiah, etc. Of course, Jesus Christ brought the power of God into a whole new era. He explained divine principles in great detail and demonstrated amazing spiritual power throughout his active 3 years of ministry. It's baffling to me that folks could witness Christ's miracles & immediately deny what they saw - they were stunned by the dimension of power they couldn't understand. Mark 3:1-6, 22 The next Biblical era of the power of God was an outpouring of the Holy Spirit we see in Acts chapter 2. That event has baffled the whole world's secular & religious communities - then and now. But it has been God's Endorsement of the New Covenant, and the Christian church.

I think the problem with God's power is that some folks will not see it unless they are looking for it. In fact, something may block the human grasp of spiritual power if people deny & contradict in unbelief, as is common today. Hello liberal thought . . . I have personally known even clergy people who are against God's power & even the resurrection of Christ. Believing those Biblical events & miracles are embarrassing to them. And that is the problem today with experiencing & understanding God's power. Without faith & believing we are blind to it, which makes God's blessing & eternal life more like a silly myth. And it's sad for people to live & die with that mindset, because according to Jesus Christ they are lost and will gravitate into that over-crowded city called hell. See "Gravity" note 98.

- "In their case the god of this world has blinded the minds of the unbelievers to keep them from seeing the light of the gospel of the glory of Christ, who is the likeness of God." 2 Corinthians 4:4
- "And without faith it is impossible to please Him. For whoever would draw near to God must believe that He exists and that He rewards those who seek Him." Hebrews 11:6
- ". . .thou hast hidden these things from the wise and understanding and revealed them to babes;" Matthew 11:25b
- "But to all who received Him, who believed in His name, he gave power to become children of God." John 1:12
- "You shall receive power when the Holy Spirit has come upon you; . . ." Acts 1:8
- "You will seek me and find me; when you seek me with all your heart," Jeremiah 29:13

Touching the power of God is a life changer for millions. I "gave it a shot" over 45 years ago to learn that my eyes were opened to God's truth, presence, & mysterious POWER. It can happen to YOU. Touching God can & will put all things in a new light, especially eternal life. Choose Jesus, He is Alive. See also "Faith", note 75.

124

LOVE & HATE

Hate is a word that has several degrees of ugly, but usually suggests passionate dislike and a feeling of enmity. Let's start with hate since there is so much of it, and it has some interesting features;

- the man hater - (misandry) There are women who deeply dislike men (I wonder why).
- the woman hater – (misogynist) This mentality a little more rare, and difficult to understand.
- the child hater - (misopedic) The 30's era comedian W.C. Fields cashed in on this attitude. He once said, [4]"I love children. Yes, if properly cooked."
- the marriage hater - (misogamy) Maybe it's why so many folks today shack-up?
- hatred of new things - (misocainea) I like old cars & distrust the new ones that are so hard to understand & fix.
- haters of reasoning - (misology or misologist) Too often people need to be challenged to think.
- jailbirds consider their guard staff to be "haters".

I try to simplify matters so here is a basic theory of hate: In the heart, people are saying "I am, and YOU are not." We tend to focus on our beautiful face, body, race, name, education, money, house, family religion, etc. Maybe just the "I am" is the root (narcissism) - self focus to an extreme, all things & everyone else suspect or objects of hate or dislike. People with this proud & natural mindset are numerous on this planet, anywhere you may go. Dealing with them is dicey because one small slip & you become a special object of their wrath, and FORGIVENESS is no option because man's fallen nature is short of that godly virtue. And sadly, even in the family the hateful spirit & grudges can last until death. People who dance with the spirit of hate are also JUDGING others to be less, which is stealing that function of judgment from God. Possibly the most incomprehensible form of hate is in that religious arena where extremists think they offer service to Allah when they kill others for being "infidels." All of the above is why Proverbs 16:5 says, "Everyone who is proud in heart is an abomination to God." See also 1 John 2:9-11 for an excellent Apostolic assessment of hate.

Now LOVE is a different "animal". Barbara Streisand sang, "People who need people (love), are the luckiest people." Whether true or not, lovers are moving toward the best team BECAUSE God is love, 1 John 4:8, and He is the biggest lover on the planet. I must include thoughts from the love chapter of the New Testament because there we find the best definition: 4. "Love is patient & kind; love is not jealous or boastful; 5. It is not arrogant or rude. Love does not insist on its own way; it is not irritable or resentful; 6. It does not rejoice at wrong, but rejoices in the right. 7. Love bears all things, believes all things, hopes all things, endures all things. 8. Love never ends; . . ." 1 Corinthians 13 Then Jesus himself said, "love one another." John 15:17 Then we come to the romantic quote of the day, [5]"Love is a fruit in season at all times, and in reach of every hand." - Mother Teresa.

Well, the Christ of the New Testament said, "you will know them by their fruit." Matthew 7:20. Can we also know ourselves by our fruit? Are the natural human instincts of pride & hate self-condemning? I suspect that very few, wish to hear God say at their final judgment "you chose to live short of my standards AND danced with hate. I saw your hissing, clicking tongue, and evil eye glare toward others too often. Depart from me to the fire that is prepared for Lucifer & his demons." (my paraphrase of Matthew 25:41.) The MUCH better plan is to make peace with God & others BEFORE that day of DIVINE judgment. Jesus and His salvation, and Holy Spirit are available & makes us love everybody - even if they are less than what we think they should be. Choose Jesus, He is Alive, and live blessed. "Behold I stand at the door and knock, if anyone hears my voice and opens the door, I will come into him and eat with him and he with me." Revelation 3:20

125

ONLY GOD COULD MAKE

Man has made a lot of amazing things. Gadgets & machines of all sizes. The airplane he invented even flies. This G-note was written at 40 thousand feet in a Singapore heavy. Then the computer that man has invented almost thinks. But for thousands of years there are things, "Only God Could Make":

- the tree - comes from a small seed & grows to great size with large & small branches in all directions.
- the natural bird - comes from an egg then lives & flies. Produces eggs that hatch the same kind of chick for the next generation.
- the fish - all kinds & sizes that again come from an egg that lies in the mud incubating for a specific time under water.
- the human eye or ear - any doctor will admit they are amazing.
- a baby animal - (or human of course) The intricate detail and cuteness is the handiwork of a capable & proud Almighty designer.
- the flower - does anyone really believe the flower made itself? See Psalm 14:1
- the Bible of history - written over a period of 1500 years or more by some 40 different authors yet has a consistent theme from cover to cover.

Now it just knocks me out how hard people work to deny the Divine creation of the tree, bird, fish, human eye, etc, then give the credit to chance - like the Webster's unabridged dictionary is the product of an explosion in a printing shop. It's almost like the human mind is desperate to avoid dealing with a Biblical & legitimate creator. Man also appears desperate to avoid the plain & simple Gospel of Jesus. I have even known Protestant & Catholic clergy people who weasel to the right & to the left in their beautiful liberalness at the Divine claims of Jesus Christ . . . I am reminded of the words of the dying witch in the famous 1939 MGM movie "The Wizard of Oz" - "Oh my Beautiful wickedness" as she melted into the ground. Consider the words of Christ, ". . . you will die in your sins (melt into the ground) unless you believe that I am He." John 8:24

Well, the short intro of this G-note only touches a few things man has made. He has also made lots of religions which suggest a path to God,

BUT man would never invent the Biblical system - "God so loved the world that He gave his only begotten son, that whoever believes on Him should not die, but have eternal life." John 3:16 and "Believe in the Lord Jesus, and you will be saved, you and your household." Acts 16:31 God invented that system of salvation BECAUSE "Only God Could Make" perfection. And for those of us who just take God at His word & try that Gospel plan - it shines "brighter & brighter until full day." Proverbs 4:18 I personally began considering Christ's Gospel 47 years ago & am still amazed by an Almighty Jesus, Revelation 1:8 & his salvation benefits. (See also "What's in It For Me" note 28)

To conclude this G-note I'd just say "Only God Could Make" the Incarnation & Gospel of Christ, AND an appeal to faith like we find in the final few pages of the Book - "Behold, I stand at the door and knock, if anyone hears my voice and opens the door I will come into him and eat with him and he with me." Revelation 3:20. Choose Jesus and His salvation. They are Alive. See also note 97 "Was Jesus God?"

126

THE PLANE CRASH

Ever since Orville & Wilbur got the first heavier than air machine off the ground in 1903, the airplane has increased in size, weight & speed. So have the crashes. Today, high-speed transportation is a massive & relatively safe industry, but what would the Wright Bros. think if they could see what they started for good & evil? The rude surprise of their "plane crashes" is amazing - the wonderful technological & expensive machine filled with humans falls out of the air & hits the ground and instantly becomes a Huge Mess of scattered & burnt debris. Now are there "plane crashes" in other arenas?

- In genuine Asian food you will have "plane crash" chicken - chopped without rhyme or reason like it flew into a brush chipper. (This G- note was written in SE Asia.)
- The U.S. entertainment industry has gone from the wholesome themes of heroism, love & virtue of the 40's & 50's to the "plane crash" picture today of profanity, sex, violence, & kinkiness.
- The music industry is now mostly a bizarre "plane crash" when you consider the lack of rhyme, melody, rhythm, & decent message or theme.
- Traditional marriage of one man & one woman is now reduced to shacking up, and "anything goes" arrangements with Supreme Court endorsement.
- American politics appears to be a "plane crash". Our early founders would all be shocked at the partisan bickering & gridlock of today.
- How about "plane crash" theology - many of our Protestant & Catholic seminaries are so liberal in "denying the Master who bought them" 2 Peter 2:1, their belief system is a scattered mess of hopeless debris, nearly devoid of saving power.
- Let's all hope & pray that planet earth doesn't get "fried" by a thermonuclear exchange. If just Russia & the U.S. released only 10% of their warheads, that would be about 1500 strikes in the northern hemisphere. A "Plane Crash" of the worst magnitude.

Well has God's original plan for his planet & humans been a successful "flight" or a "plane crash"?? The garden beginning as recorded in Genesis 1-3 did not go well. Then we see the total decline of humanity only a few chapters later, and the flood of Noah to annihilate our rebellious race & it's sin. A couple thousand years later we see Moses coming down from a mountain top meeting with God, only to find Israel partying like hell. He smashed the first 2 tablets of the Ten Commandments in frustration, Exodus 32:19. (That was early writing by the way – 1500 or more BC.) The times of the Judges & Kings show dramatically how the chosen people struggled with growth & development; then disobedience, apostasy, & decline - a series of "plane crashes". God brought in their promised Messiah on schedule Malachi 3:1, but He was condemned to death by the highest court of the land - the Sanhedrin. The most amazing & dark "plane crash" event of history, Matthew 27:41-51. And the magnitude of that event is identified by our very calendar - BC & AD. We now live in "The year of the Lord" AD 2016.

Even though our world has had "plane crash" disasters in every arena from the beginning, I am encouraged that God is big enough to ultimately have things under control. I don't lose sleep worrying that I'll be vaporized in a rude accident or nuclear war. (See "Rude Surprises" Note 79) But I am thankful for the Salvation of Jesus Christ that brings peace & hope to individuals like myself. Have you connected?

- Psalms 37:4 "Take delight in the Lord and He will give you the desires of your heart."
- Isaiah 53:5 "He was wounded for our transgressions, he was bruised for our iniquities; upon him was the chastisement that made us whole, and with his stripes we are healed." (The Gospel according to Isaiah – 700 years B.C.)
- John 10:27 "My sheep hear my voice, and I know them, and they follow me."
- Hebrews 2:3 "How shall we escape if we neglect such a great salvation? It was declared at first by the Lord, and it was attested to us by those who heard him,"

With the Biblical connection above, we can live in the victory in spite of the chaotic & declining world around us. See "Mindset of Victory" note 103. I discovered the Lord over 44 years ago & know He is faithful & true to His Word. Choose Jesus, He is Alive. You will be blessed in the Christian value system, and thru the endless ages of eternity.

127

SANTA CLAUS

Santa Claus trivia – Why is Christmas day like any other day at the office? Because you do all the work & the fat guy gets all the credit. OR Why is Santa Claus always a man? Because a woman would never wear the same outfit every year. OR Three stages of men: believes in Santa Claus, doesn't believe in Santa, then BECOMES Santa Clause. Well the legend of S.C. has Dutch roots. From about 1765 he was Sinterklaas, or Saint Nicholas, St. Nick, etc. The fat man in red suit brings toys & good cheer each year on Dec 25. There may have been a benevolent figure that gave gifts to children in Dutch legend, but the flying reindeer & sleigh has been added. However loved or maligned Santa may be, Christmas & Santa have to be a good thing:

- As a holiday, children are completely enthused.
- Adults also get cheered up from the kid's <u>wonderful</u> attitude.
- Lots of people get an extra day off close to the New Year's holiday.
- Economies are stimulated by purchasing toys & gifts. Many stores make their best profits in Nov. & Dec.
- Then Christmas music is enchanting for all to enjoy.

I like ALL of the Christmas stuff because it is originally a Biblical connection, and the grand scale of it anchors the name of Christ in millions of minds – even in that Muslim city Kuala Lumpur, Malaysia (December '15) they get enchanted with our Christmas. Matthew 2:1-12 is the <u>Biblical</u> connection, and the gifts & materialism speaks to me of the GIVING NATURE of GOD. Lucky for us, our Biblical God is <u>gracious</u>, <u>benevolent</u>, & <u>GIVING</u>. Now if Santa Claus or Saint Nic can be seen as <u>a type of Christ</u>, then what gifts does He bring?

- God in Christ gives/created our earth & keeps it balanced in its orbit around the sun. Genesis 1:1, John 1:1 (Those two refs. are a lot like Christianity 101.)
- Christ in God gives life – even if it's not as perfect as we might wish. Hebrews 1:3a
- He gives nourishment, music & happiness to most folks. Colossians 2:9-10
- God in Christ gives Christmas. Isaiah 9:6 "For unto us a child is born, to us a son is given; and the government will be upon his shoulder,

and his name will be called "Wonderful, Counselor, Mighty God, Everlasting Father, Prince of Peace." KJV

- He gives/reveals answers about the purpose of life & destiny of souls to those who want God's answers. See "What is the Answer?" note 41.
- He gives Himself as salvation from sin; He gives God's blessing & eternal life to those who seek Him. Jeremiah 29:13 "You will seek me and find me; when you seek me with all your heart."

Well I know that Jesus Christ as Santa Claus is a repulsive thought to some, but I try to look beyond the materialism of Christmas towards the giver of all things - the Lord God of Scripture. And that Scripture reveals God as Father, Son, and Holy Spirit - one God in three persons. So Santa Claus as "the Son" is only good theology, and an allegorical picture to help illustrate the giving nature of God. And the list of "goodies" above is NOTHING compared to the thousands of promises we find in the Book - if we read & believe it . . . (if we don't, we are cheating ourselves.)

Whether Jesus Christ wears a red suit or a white robe, we are still accountable to Him. People should consider the solemn words of Christ, "I am the way, and the truth, and the life; no one comes to the Father, but by me." And these also "Take delight in the Lord, and he will give you the desires of your heart." Choose Jesus, He is Alive. Those last refs. are John 14:6 and Psalm 37:4. See also note 97 "Was Jesus God?"

128

THE KAMIKAZE COWBOY *

The two characters above should be well known. The Kamikaze was a Japanese pilot of late WWII who was trained to fly small airplanes with a big bomb into U.S. ships. My wife and I have been to Kagoshima Japan where the famous Kamikaze's are from. Then the cowboy is a character who loves the horse and makes it a part of his lifestyle. We live in the Verde Valley of Arizona which has some cowboys for sure. One owns a rodeo arena & manages his concrete redi-mix company having six or so full-size C. trucks - Randy even drives (class act).

We recently met the combination of the two characters above. George Kamiawa is a Japanese musician of rare multi-instrument talent, living & performing in Australia of all places. His "country" style stage show revealed the kind of originality, focus, outrageous presence, determination, sense of humor, and precision that wins the title of "Kamikaze Cowboy." Well as a Bible student for over 45 years I see some characters in the Book who romp & stomp & impress me the same way. (Hopefully using the K. C. label above for them is not blasphemous.)

- Moses - What a glaring example of God's presence with a human all the way to fulfillment of the Divine will & purpose. Exodus thru Deuteronomy – about 140 pages of premium Old Testament miracles AND Divine dictation.
- David the shepherd/king and of course Elijah. Elijah is unique in that he didn't experience physical death but was taken out in a "flaming chariot." 2 Kings 2
- Isaiah was a statesman & prophet so rare he wrote with precision much of the Gospel of Christ 700 years before Christ appeared in the flesh. See Isaiah chapters 53 & 55
- Jesus was a Biblical "Kamikaze Cowboy" of the RAREST order. On His suicide mission he was Bold as a Lion, speaking to THOUSANDS at a time, walking on water, raising the dead, challenging established tradition, etc. How about His willing execution for the benefit of others? The" cowboy" with pistols on his belt? He said to his adversaries, "you will die in your sins unless you believe I am He" John 8:24
- The Apostle Paul - This guy had focus & determination that caught even God's attention (see Acts 9). He was overcome & knocked senseless by a Divine encounter & change that resulted in lots of miracles, and

intellectually defining MUCH of Christ's mission & purpose. About one third of the New Testament came to us thru Paul.

When I think of the fascinating Book that has been given to us by writers like those above, AND my own experience with Christ's salvation for over 45 years, I wonder if the nature & character of God Himself isn't close to the title of this Gospel-note. I truly see originality, focus, outrageous presence, determination, precision, and even humor between the covers of the Bible. The true God is certainly not a casual character, and His Book is not a casual book.

For those who believe and give its Gospel message a chance (or a try), it is the Answer to this crazy and hard world. "O taste & see that the Lord is good, blessed is the man who trusteth in Him." Psalm 34:8 KJV And, as we walk with the Lord thru His Book & world, we begin to realize what kind of Amazing Person our Biblical God is and always was. Then the Second Coming of Christ to cleanse & judge sin at all levels will truly be a "Kamikaze Cowboy" operation evident to all & "outrageous". This world of intellectual denial & false religions won't stand a chance. Choose Jesus, He is Alive . . . See also "The Names of Christ" note 46 for more insight into the character of the Lord.

* The title of this G-NOTE may be a little controversial but so are notes 82, 88, & 122.

129

REINCARNATION

This is an old concept and popular in Hindu religious teaching. It basically means that the soul is reborn in another body for a second go at life. Maybe in a different kind of species – some believe Divine punishment can cause a person to re-appear as a lower animal or insect. Going the other way, one may do well in life & reappear in a better time or place or class of society. Now reincarnation seems to be a popular thing that many refer to, even in Judeo Christian cultures.

As a Bible student I wanted to know what Scripture says about reincarnation. Well, my search came up nearly empty. Even a determined look at current & past Biblical reference books are amazingly blank on the subject of reincarnation. It may well be that TRUTH comes from legitimate Scripture, which is the Bible of history. Reincarnation is not truth, so it is not found in the Bible. And the early church fathers (85 – 350 A.D.) such as Justin Martyr, Tatian, Athenagoras, Tertullian, and others all taught reincarnation is a false doctrine. Irenaeus said, "R. is absurd".

So why would people go for a notion that says they can come back for a second try at life? It has to do with JUDGMENT. It is well known that the Bible and the Church (Protestant & Catholic) teach that God holds all accountable & has a serious & sober day for every soul at the end of their life. Revelation 20:12-13 is as blunt as a spoon. And for God to be Just & Fair, that judgment is MANDATORY & FINAL. People being cunning & devious by nature find excuses for the JUDGMENT problem. Reincarnation sweetens it by putting it off or expecting a second chance. Now I know people believe what they want to believe, BUT what if reincarnation is only an illusion, or false hope??

THEN folks delay or reject the Salvation & promises of the New Covenant. They put more stock in the natural thought of Gurus & atheists and insult the inspiration & hope of God's Word. They live without the favor & blessing of God in a difficult world. They personally miss all the Divine goodies of this life, AND what has been prepared for them in glory. They face that Judgment Day totally un-prepared and naked in the presence of a Holy God. Ecclesiastes 5:15 Then they have to eat that judgment that Jesus died to "cover" for them. And they create a blank space in the circle of their saved family members in Heaven. What a shame to forfeit all to such an "old bone" as reincarnation. [6]"No road to perdition has ever been more thronged than that of false doctrine. Error is a shield over the conscience and a bandage over the eyes." D.C. Hodge

As far as choosing non-Biblical thought (and lies of our adversary), the Scripture is not silent:

- Proverbs 19:27 "Cease, my son, to hear the instruction that causeth to err from the words of knowledge."
- Ecclesiastes 11:3b "if a tree falls to the south or to the north, in the place where the tree falls, there it will lie."
- John 5:24 "Truly, truly, I say to you, he who hears my word and believes him who sent me, has eternal life; he does not come into judgment, but has passed from death to life." Jesus Christ said that.
- Colossians 2:8 "Beware lest any man spoil you through philosophy and vain deceit, after the tradition of men, and after the rudiments of the world, and not after Christ."
- ** Hebrews 9:27 "It is appointed unto men ONCE to die, but after this the judgment."

- H. Lindsell – [7]"Truth shall forever be on the scaffold, and wrong forever on the throne as long as time shall last."

I totally believe all folks should do some homework to challenge their assumptions on the afterlife. A quality study Bible can often be had for about $2 at a thrift store. Of course, a Bible believing church will explain the case also. Choose Jesus and his Word, they are Alive and ABLE to get folks on the right track. Reincarnation is a dead horse, and only able to produce "Rude Surprises" (note 79). See also "New Age" note 56.

130

OPTIMISTIC CONNECTIONS

We were recently in the USO at the Honolulu Airport waiting for a flight home. On a wall I noticed several artistic placards with the optimistic thoughts below neatly presented:

- Life isn't about how to survive the storm, but how to dance in the rain.
- Live fully, challenge yourself, be kind & generous, inspire someone, be grateful. Take the road less traveled – it's never too late.
- Dance as though no one is watching, love as though you have never loved before, sing as though no one can hear you, live as though heaven is on earth.
- Be thankful, believe, live life, cherish love, dare to dream, have faith.
- May our home know happiness, each room hold laughter, and every window open to possibilities.

While we were there on Oahu and drove around that "island paradise" (?) I also noticed lots of homeless people in parks & beaches, & along highways living in lean-to's & small tents kind of like animals. Many of them were native Hawaiians "priced out of paradise." So what about "Optimistic Connections" when folks are down & out, or young & just not able to "connect" with anything – love, money, comfort, peace, happiness, success, or direction of any kind? Is there a mindset of victory & hope that makes the wall slogans above more reality, & not just elusive optimism? Enter the Biblical/Christian faith & value system which produces a kind of peace & stability – THAT is the mindset of victory for millions in every place & age.

- Psalm 94:11 "The Lord God is a sun and shield; he bestows favor and honor. No good thing does the Lord withhold from those who walk uprightly."
- Jeremiah 6:16 "Thus says the Lord: "Stand by the roads and look, and ask for the ancient paths, where the good way is; and walk in it and find rest for your souls."
- Jeremiah 29:11 "I know the plans I have for you, says the Lord, plans for welfare and not for evil, to give you a future and a hope."
- John 3:16 "For God so loved the world that he gave his only Son, that

whoever believes in him should not perish but have eternal life."

- John 14:6 KJV Jesus saith unto him, "I am the way, the truth, and the life: no man cometh unto the Father, but by me."
- Philippians 4:13 KJV "I can do all things through Christ which strengtheneth me."

While we were in that Airport USO it was inspiring to see those wall placard slogans. But it is God that gives each person the ability to realize those fine goals & ideals. Without His touch & Spirit, we may try in vain. Now Christianity is not necessarily a magic pill to solve all the personal & world problems out there, but those who are open to the Gospel of Christ have the inside track on receiving Divine anointing & blessing. And that leads to the best version of ourselves. That's been my experience & observation of over 45 years. Choose Jesus & His value system, they are alive. See also "The Endorsement" & "The Mindset of Victory" notes 15 and 103.

131

HAZARDS OF GIVING

Giving is a hard core & clearly taught spiritual law or principle of Christianity. Giving is not easy, but it does test God's principles. It's a place many folks just don't go – they might talk about it, but little action. I personally started giving at the beginning of my "renewal" in Christ Feb '72 & learned that the Word is true on this subject – what we give does come back, as a rule. Luke 6:38. And Christ did say, "It is more blessed to give than to receive." Acts 20:35. This means we are expected to practice giving. But what about the hazards?

As with other principles of Christianity (there are about 10 or so, see note 180), giving requires a certain mindset. That is to do what one believes is right, even though others will question our motives. And we may question our own motives. It may be abusive too – titles like fool, sucker, busybody, do-gooder, religious maniac, etc. can echo in the giver's mind. I think this is why many would–be givers don't give, fearing self rejection, & wounded pride & ego. (Of course, our adversary himself is a ruthless accuser). Practical hazard #1 in this world of distrust is being double crossed. That's where a gift or good deed is done, then the recipient spitefully reacts for unknown reasons. P. H. #2 is giving to a friend or charity – they may be ingrates & act like you didn't give enough or anything at all. P. H. #3 is giving too regular so that the gift becomes a "bill" that is almost owed them. (No wonder Scrooge was so tight). It's wise to not expect any reciprocation from a receiver, AND only in the parameters of Faith expect a response/return from the resources & timing of God. See note 75.

Personally, I had seen MUCH rewards of giving, but was prevented from seeing the worst "Hazards of Giving" until about 12 years into the faith. Amazingly it was a minister that proved to be quite treacherous. (See "Imposters" note 57.) Now the Bible is a book of reality, and Hazards of Giving are revealed there too. Joash was a king of Judah from birth. Only his grandmother Athaliah wanted the kingdom for herself & killed all her grandsons immediately when her son died – king Ahaziah. The priest Jehoiada hid baby Joash for 6 years in the temple, or he would have been "slain" too. Jehoiada promoted Joash's crowning at age 7 & helped him to rule for 40 years. But when the priest died, Joash had his son killed. That is rotten gratitude, which is a common "Hazard of Giving".

See 2 Chronicles 23-24.

Of course, the experience of Jesus Christ shows the Hazards of Giving. Who in this hard world has given more than Our Lord as He went around Palestine healing the sick & lame, replacing blind eyes, feeding thousands with miracle power, raising dead back to life, teaching folks how to be successful in life & death, then in the Atonement for the sins of the world – John 3:16–19? That persecution, rejection, and terrible death was "hazardous" – "to the max." And the 12 Apostles were nearly all martyred for their similar giving lifestyle & preaching. But in the final analysis, who's shoes would we rather be in when Divine rewards are given out?? The giver's or the taker's?? And my 44 years of Christian experience is that Divine rewards come all along the way in the form of answered prayer, special "goodies", & God's blessing. See "Seed Faith" note 109. "Knowing that whatever good anyone does, he will receive the same again from the Lord . . ." Ephesians 6:8

Well to finish this tough subject, I'll just say this world has always bashed God's principles, but they still hold true. We might do well in the art of giving to be discrete & anonymous whenever possible – "don't let the left hand know what the right is doing." – Jesus Christ, Matthew 6:3. The Hazards of Giving can be minimized that way. Here is a reflection from an old dead saint, J. Oswald Sanders:

When I am dying how glad I shall be
That the lamp of my life has been blazed out for Thee.
I shall be glad in whatever I gave,
Labor, or money, one sinner to save;
I shall not mind that the path has been rough,
That Thy dear feet led the way is enough.

Choose Jesus and His value system, they are Alive. See also "Christian Giving" note 30.

132

DIVINE HEALING

The roots of this "mystery" go back at least 3500 years to the time of Moses. Exodus 23:25 "So you shall serve the Lord your God, and He will bless your bread and your water. And I will take sickness away from the midst of you." Of course, that's a Biblical reference which blocks today's Darwin crowd. But for those who have FAITH, the roots of Divine Healing are plenteous. Deuteronomy 7:15, Psalm 107:20, Isaiah 53:5, Jeremiah 30:17, Matthew 8:16-17, Mark 16:17-18, and of course Hebrews 13:8 tells us "Jesus Christ is the same yesterday, today, and forever." And if Jesus Christ is the "author of life", with "all power" today, then Divine Healing is no problem. Jesus did a lot of healings during his 3 yr. ministry, then told his disciples, "Truly, truly, I say to you, he who believes in me will also do the works that I do; and greater works than these will he do, because I go to the Father." John 14:12

Well, I personally didn't know much about the Biblical roots of Divine Healing in Army basic training, but I had a terrible flat foot problem which caused me to pray in desperation. Some kind of mysterious strength just flowed thru the pain while I was marching & I was able to continue on. That convinced me. See "My Miracles" note 33. I experienced and witnessed other D.H. as a young believer in Christ. Years later my elderly aunt shared her Divine Healing story. She was in the convent preparing to be a nun when T.B. got her lungs – about 1940. Her mother & those nuns prayed for her healing which came to pass. She couldn't stay in the convent so got married but was advised by doctors not to have children. Well, she had a healthy nine, and lived to be 87.

<u>For the sake of inspiration</u> there are two cases of Divine Healing in the gospels which seemed to challenge even Jesus Christ. Those are the daughter of Jairus, a synagogue leader, Mark chapter 5, and Lazarus, a personal friend of Jesus, John chapter 11. Both times Christ wasn't able to get to the sick soon enough & <u>they died</u> waiting for his visit. How sad – but according to Scripture Jesus raised both back to life. That's way beyond healing in my opinion. Maybe the message is this – if Jesus Christ is involved, you're covered even if "worse comes to worse". Now I <u>want to believe these</u> awesome stories because believing the WORD is the essence of saving faith. Too many today want to scoff at the WORD & its truth which kills faith, and blocks divine healing, or getting anything else from God.

<u>For the sake of reality</u>, where is Divine Healing when folks have prayed & believed to no avail? God's response to any prayer request is either yes, no, or

wait. We should BELIEVE for healing because it is a benefit of being Christian and EXPECT to receive. But if there is no evidence of the good stuff, maybe God's answer is "no". He is sovereign, so that's His option. I prayed believing for eye healing early on & my eyes stayed blurry & I continued wearing glasses. But a couple years later my glasses saved my eyes from molten lead which shot in my face. But other healings I have received. Some just take time. I believe we should pray for our healing needs first. After a reasonable time (different for all), then go to the doctor. But even then, Divine Healing isn't done – God is able to bless the hands & mind of that doc. I suppose missionaries & poor folks that have minimum medical available would be in a higher priority with God for D.H. . . . But God can heal today, - anyone, any place, any time. (Especially when standard medical is mainly about <u>money</u>.)

The best shot for any <u>believer</u> who needs & wants Divine Healing is to apply the scriptural formula:

- "According to your faith be it done to you." Jesus said that, Matthew 9:29
- "Draw near to God and He will draw near to you" James 4:8a
- "Is anyone among you sick? Let him call for the elders of the church, and let them pray over him, anointing him with oil in the name of the Lord. And the prayer of faith will save the sick, and the Lord will raise him up. And if he has committed sins, he will be forgiven." James 5:14-15

In today's world that board of elders might throw ice water on the seekers faith if <u>they</u> don't believe in Divine Healing. That's why it's important to be in a Bible believing church. To receive Divine Healing, we need to be close to Christ and His Word. Choose Jesus, He is Alive.

133

THE FLYING WOODSTOVE

I like woodstoves. Even had a small shop in Oklahoma & made a few of them. Recently I took the ugliest one of five on hand & made it into a piece of yard art. It's mounted upside down on top of a mobile home axle & is balanced with five paddles to catch the wind. It has a flying scorpion above it to complete the charm. My caption in front says, "As the Whirled Burns."

There is actually some good theology (perhaps a bit negative), represented by this "Flying Woodstove", especially in this late hour of world history. As the woodstove above is a burning large object, so is the earth with all of its wars, suffering & death. And as my "stove" is balanced in the air & turns, so does the earth in space. The "upside down" speaks of the bizarre age we are living in. Then the flying scorpion is an end time agent of God's wrath. Revelation Chapter 9.

As a Bible student, I've tried to avoid the end of time predictions we find in Old Testament prophesy, & the Apocalypse teaching in the New Testament. But a notable & prolific Biblical scholar Dr. Tim La Haye has an excellent book called "Are We Living in the End Times?" (copyright 1999, which only means it's later still.) Now there are 4 main schools of Revelation: <u>Preterist</u> – its mysterious content done early – 300-400 years after Christ. <u>Historical</u> – its content done over the last 1900 years or so. <u>Spiritual</u> – its content is meant to be taken symbolically of the good vs. evil spiritual conflict in this world. Then the <u>Futural School</u> – the events of the last days of Earth as we know it. Dr. La Haye has done a great job explaining Revelation & many other related parts of Scripture in the Futural school of thought – <u>that we are close to the end of time</u>. That "end times" interpretation of Old & New Testament Scripture <u>clearly</u> teaches:

- A general decline of godly standards globally "As it were in the days of Noah, so will be the coming of the Son of man." Matthew 24:37
- The rapture of the Church, - The "Blessed Hope" this is the <u>hardcore</u> element of Christian doctrine that says all Christians will be taken out BEFORE all hell breaks loose. But it is previewed by the translation of Elijah 2 Kings 2, and Christ himself after His resurrection & witnessed by 500 people. For the nutshell reference see Thessalonians 4:16-17, but other glimpses of this doctrine are

Isaiah 26:20 "Come, my people, enter your chambers, and shut your doors behind you; hide yourselves for a little while until the wrath is past." Matthew 24:40-41 "Then two men will be in the field; one is taken and one left. Two women will be grinding at the mill; one is taken, and one is left."

- Seven years of TRIBULATION worldwide, with disease, famine, fast moving wars, etc. Jesus said, "If those days had not been shortened, no human being would be saved; but for the sake of the elect those days will be shortened." Matthew 24:22 That 7 years of various judgments of God worldwide is ordained to purge sin & hate from planet earth. Revelation chapters 6-16
- 144,000 Jews promoting a global REVIVAL with extreme satanic opposition. Matthew 24:14, Revelation 7
- Resurrected Moses & Elijah (my view of who those "two witnesses" are. See Matthew 17), in the streets of Jerusalem in the face of world view – TV cameras?? Revelation 11
- The charismatic Antichrist world leader that proclaims himself to be God. Daniel 11 & Revelation 13
- Then a major attack on Israel resulting in the "battle of Armageddon", where Christ's angelic forces are victorious. Luke 21:20, Rev. 19
- Finally, the physical return of Jesus Christ "The Glorious Appearing" to set up His 1000 year peaceful & prosperous reign according to prophecy. Isaiah 11, Micah 4, Zechariah 8 & 14, Revelation 20

So especially in the last days, "The Flying Woodstove", or "As the Whirled Burns" is only good theology. I know many prefer not to believe such hard-to-believe and dramatic concepts as the above, but if the world had a miraculous beginning, why wouldn't it have a miraculous end?? Does God have no style? (I think He has a lot of style! Just no competition, see note 102.) And this planet is clearly overpopulated with ungodly & hateful humans – why wouldn't God end it dramatically?? I have studied the Scriptures for at least 45 years, & the Biblical drama of the end is more credible to me now than ever before. And basically, the message of ALL end-time prophecy is simply that our Biblical God finally wins. What's wrong with that? Well, "As the Whirled Burns", whose team are you on, God's or the World's?? Jesus said, "I am the way, and the truth, and the life; no one comes to the Father, but by me." John 14:6 Choose Jesus, He is Alive.

134

THE DEATH SENTENCE

The U.S. Court System has an interesting history. Starting at least from 1776, then with our constitution's 6th amendment which guarantees a speedy trial, there is supposed to be "liberty & justice for all." Well, it's not always clear who does the thinking, but it is clear that today one will surely not get a speedy trial, & justice may not happen either. Lots of convicted murderers get easier sentences than certain other offences. (And the death sentence may soon be banned by the Supreme Court, forcing taxpayers to support those murderers as they live a long life in expensive jails.)

Now in a legitimate theocracy, God is doing the thinking which at least makes a striking contrast with man's best efforts. How about the Mosaic Law of maybe 3500 years ago? Does it compare with today's "death sentence"? Here are some offences that would and did get folks terminated (swiftly at that): Murder-Genesis 9:6, Cursing one's Mother or Father-Leviticus 20:9, Adultery & Incest-Leviticus 20:10-12, Homosexuality-Leviticus 20:13, Witchcraft-Leviticus 20:27, Blasphemy-Leviticus 24:16, Violating the Sabbath-Numbers 15:32-36. And the code of Moses stresses accountability in the 5th chapter of Leviticus, "If any one sins, doing any of the things which the Lord has commanded not to be done, though he does not know it, yet he is guilty and shall bear his iniquity." v.17

The severe penalties of the above sins may be hard to understand, especially when compared with today's liberal sentencing. Of course, it was the age of Biblical LAW to get a brand-new Godly nation started on the "right track". But mostly that LAW was revealed to Moses to show the world of all ages what a holy God thinks of SIN. Christ came along after centuries of grand scale failures of God's people, to offer the world and all individuals a solution, or expiation for our sin. Only we have to BELIEVE in Christ to get that solution.

The first coming of Christ about 2000 years ago changed a lot of things, including "the death sentence". The brainiest chosen writer of the New Testament said this "Now we are discharged from the Law, dead to that which held us captive, so that we serve not under the old written code but in the new life of the Spirit." Romans 7:6 The New Covenant does deal with the death sentence, but more in a spiritual sense – the physical sense is left to civil authorities. Romans 13:1-4

So, it appears that the Old Testament LAW gives us clear examples of a holy God's attitude towards sin. The New Covenant (especially in the book of Romans) shows how sin can separate us from favor with God, then Divine displeasure, & wrath for eternity (spiritual death or hell). That New Covenant also speaks of grace which is the other side of LAW. "But God, who is rich in mercy, out of the great love with which he loved us, even when we were dead through our trespasses, made us alive together with Christ (by grace you have been saved)," Ephesians 2:4-5 And Grace is not fair – we have all done some of the things in the "death sentence" list above which got Moses' era sinners executed. By the rules of Old Covenant law, we deserve nothing good either, only condemnation, because we are still dealing with the same God. Then today we have a callous attitude toward sin and wholesale quantities of it, "because sentence against an evil deed is not executed speedily, the heart of the sons of men is fully set to do evil." Ecclesiastes 8:11

The age of GRACE is so much easier for sinners. God has made provisions for us to beat sin & it's penalties. It's sad when folks turn away from God's authorized salvation, preferring other (Christ rejecting) belief systems. The wiser approach is to accept Christ without delay or filibuster. Choose Jesus, He is Alive. And let "the death sentence" of any kind take care of itself. See also "Death Bed Confessions" note 86.

135

IS FUNDAMENTALISM BAD?

First a definition of Fundamentalism would be in order – from "The Religion Book", pg. 228, 2004 by Jim Willis. ". . . the word conjures up two images. The first is the old image of the Protestant Christian fundamentalist – the 'Bible believing, virgin birth, born again, second coming' image. The second and more recent image is that of the Islamic fundamentalist." And any Fundamentalist is just someone who accepts his faith's basic doctrines.

Now that doesn't seem like such a bad thing unless it's the kind of faith that attacks fundamentalists & kills others in the name of Allah . . . In the Christian sense we have lots of groups that are Fundamentalist oriented. Baptist, Pentecostal, Gospel groups, and a variety of others are considered fundamentalists. When I found the Lord in '72 (or did He find me??) the word Fundamentalist was not an issue. I wasn't impressed with any kind of religion as such – Sunday meetings, ritual, right attitude, etc., but the presence of the Holy Spirit, miracles, divine guidance, answered prayer, etc., was pretty neat stuff. My experiment with Christianity was just like those folks I read about in the Bible. I began to like what I had touched, & if it was Fundamentalism, I didn't care.

I think in our day people have disconnected from accountability to God & religious principles because science seems to disapprove. Therefore, fundamentalism has become a word with a bad image. And folks use the common rejection of the image of Fundamentalism as an excuse to reject the Word of God & it's Author. Many of them don't examine those elements of Fundamentalism – "Bible believing, virgin birth, born again, second coming" – if it's fundamentalism it must be bad just because. And besides, C. Darwin & Steve Hawking wouldn't approve of this stuff . . . Well, I resolved from the start in '72 to read the Book thoroughly & carefully. My missionary friend D.L. gave me a golden rule then – "if you find something in the Bible you don't understand or find especially credible, just go on. It will clarify later." And God has blessed my experience with those miracles & good things mentioned in paragraph 2 above – for about 47 years now.

So "Is Fundamentalism Bad?", no Fundamentalism is a good thing, only some extreme forms of it may be a little intense, but in Christianity that's not so bad. Better to be too Fundamentalist & approved by Him – "Then the King will say to those at his right hand, "Come, O blessed of my

Father, inherit the kingdom prepared for you from the foundation of the world;" Matthew 25:34, than to be without principles & liberal, and hear Christ say, "Depart from me, you cursed, into the eternal fire prepared for the devil and his angels;" Matthew 25:41 Why challenge God? Better to take on a 400 lb. gorilla. The best approach is to study the Word & see if it's false. Many have done this to find it's true! – I did . . . I conclude that the spirit of this age has branded F. & Bible thumping as bad which BLOCKS many from studying the WORD, which they need to make an informed decision for Christ & those fundamentals. "Judging a book by its cover??" "The blind leading the blind??" Here's a few references from "the fundamentalist handbook":

- ". . .the god of this world has blinded the minds of the unbelievers, to keep them from seeing the light of the gospel of the glory of Christ, who is the likeness of God." 2 Corinthians 4:4
- "Study to shew thyself approved unto God, a workman that needeth not to be ashamed, rightly dividing the word of truth." 2 Timothy 2:15 KJV
- "Now these Jews were more noble than those in Thessalonica, for they received the word with all eagerness, examining the Scriptures daily to see if these things were so." Acts 17:11
- "Being born again, not of corruptible seed, but of incorruptible, by the word of God, which liveth and abideth forever." 1 Peter 1:23 KJV
- "Men of Galilee, why do you stand looking into heaven? This Jesus, who was taken up from you into heaven, will come in the same way as you saw him go into heaven." Acts 1:11 (The word of two angels when the resurrected Christ ascended.)

Choose Jesus, He is Alive, and probably the original fundamentalist. See "Was Jesus God?" note 97.

136

COMFORT FROM ABOVE

This Old world is a place where people sometimes look for comfort. They start out looking to Mom; and most folks find it there. Then at an early age we look for friendship & acceptance for comfort. Of course, at some point young people find out about alcohol. In the South (and elsewhere) it might be Southern Comfort, 88 proof . . .? (I had a dear sister who became addicted to booze early in her life – her stomach rotted & ¾ of it was removed at age 35 or so. Then her throat rotted & a festering hole developed, & at age 72 was her demise, without "comfort"). In the north people get comfort from warm & cozy coats & sleeping bags. And getting our comfort from this world & its natural sources may be fine & good. Only the reliability & durability of that comfort can often disappoint, or completely fail – the frozen boot in the jaw can happen when we need something more soothing & warm . . .

But how does "Comfort From Above" work? I believe God has put us on this planet to seek Him, and the kind of comfort this world doesn't offer. Jesus said, "Peace I leave with you; my peace I give to you; not as the world gives do I give to you. Let not your hearts be troubled, neither let them be afraid." John 14:27 Well that should be comforting, and it is from Truth Incarnate Himself. But are there other references in the Book on the subject of "Comfort From Above"? Yes, from cover to cover, please let me offer a few:

- Deuteronomy 31:8 "It is the Lord who goes before you; he will be with you; he will not fail you or forsake you; do not fear or be dismayed." (Moses said that to Joshua a General, but also valid for the ordinary seeker today.)
- Ezra 8:22a "The hand of our God is for good upon all that seek him, . . ."
- Psalms 25:14 KJV "The secret of the Lord is with them that fear him, and he will shew them his covenant".
- Psalms 94:19 "When the cares of my heart are many, thy consolations cheer my soul."
- Lamentations 3:25 "The Lord is good to those who wait for him, to the soul that seeks him."
- Romans 8:18 "I consider that the sufferings of this present time are not worth comparing with the glory that is to be revealed to us."

- Romans 8:28 KJV "We know that all things work together for good to them that love God, to them who are called according to his purpose."
- 1 Corinthians 1:3 KJV ". . . God of all comfort."
- Numbers 6:24-26 "The Lord bless you and keep you; The Lord make his face to shine upon you, and be gracious to you; The Lord lift up his countenance upon you, and give you peace." (That is the great benediction of Moses – famous for thirty-five hundred years now, and still valid.)

Those references are too many for an essay of this length. But they are morsels of truth I've had memorized for about 40 years! Back then I discovered many elements of Divine provision for distraught people (myself one of them), and developed an interest in the "Comfort From Above". I have found that God's principles & provisions are reliable & steady, & basically free. It's just too sad that most folks don't know (or care) about the good stuff from our Biblical God. I want to be one that spreads the good news. And note 28 also deals with Divine provisions – "What's In It For Me?"

Now Scripture teaches that the natural human condition is unsaved & short of God's favor or blessing. Romans 3:23 Some folks can't handle this Biblical teaching & cook up all kinds of reasons why they think it's not so. But for those of us who just accept the Word as it is, we are in a much better position to receive good stuff, & "Comfort From Above". Jesus puts it in a nutshell in the third chapter of Revelation, v. 20 "Behold, I stand at the door and knock; if any one hears my voice and opens the door, I will come in to him and eat with him, and he with me." Choose God's salvation & Jesus, they are Alive. Be on the winning team and get your share of that "Comfort From Above". See also note 103 "Mindset of Victory" & note 157 "Happy Facts of Life".

137

EVIDENCE OF BEING LOST

According to Scripture, humans are either lost or found. In the Old Testament the Jewish race was the "chosen" or found race. In the New Testament, Christ re-defines being "found" more in a personal commitment context than a racial or national framework. In Matthew chapter 7 (which is an excellent assessment of lost & found), we read the words of Jesus himself, "you will know them by their fruits . . . every sound tree bears good fruit, but the bad tree bears evil fruit," vs. 16-17. So, what does that "evil fruit" or "evidence" look like?? The following list is by no means complete:

- Having no need or interest in the Church Jesus Christ died for. Lots of folks are in this boat . . .
- Having no need or respect for the Bible which God has prepared for our instruction & comfort.
- Using profanity, & God's name in vain is evidence of being on the "lost" team.
- Movie going & TV to an excess. The theatre has always been suspect by the religious community & today it's too easy to see why. I personally believe many movie directors & TV barons are possessed by high level demons of hell. The Amish have a healthy (maybe extreme?) position to totally reject the movies, & TV is taboo to them also.
- Bars & drinking needs little comment – but specialty bars appear to be worse. Especially LGBT – too bizarre. God will at best have 3 words for it. "Depart from me . . ." Matthew 25:41 See note 34 "Diabolic Churches."
- There has always been those who make fun & jokes about Divine material – heaven, hell, angels, devils, etc. That kind of levity & entertainment smells like "evidence" to me.
- Then we have the intellectual crowd that says, "all paths lead to the same heaven." I know it appears bigoted to believe "one-way Jesus", but that other position dumps on Biblical revelation AND the words of Christ. Either the Bible is true or it's not . . . Hebrews 4:12-13 gives a penetrating assessment of the Word – both Christ & the written pages.
- A focus on one's personal integrity, staying out of jail, paying one's way, environmental concerns & activism, animal rights, etc. – all of which may be fine & good, but the criterion for acceptance w/God

is accepting Jesus Christ & His atonement for our sin & humanness. "There is a way which seemeth right unto a man, but the end thereof are the ways of death." Proverbs 14:12 KJV

Maybe the best evidence of being lost is that argument that says, "I don't need to be found if there is NO LOST" -or- "there is no devil or hell to worry about." People who say those things are <u>exactly</u> where the god of this fallen world wants them – lost & happy about it. Well it's a sad day for this country to see such numbers displaying the "evidence" listed above. (And I know this is a negative type of "G-note", but it needed to be written – especially to balance the one before, note 136 "Comfort From Above.") Below are a few references from God's word which seem to shed light on this sad subject:

- "Rescue those who are being taken away to death; hold back those who are stumbling to the slaughter." Proverbs 24:11 (The preacher's job.)
- "Jesus said . . . "if you continue in my word, you are truly my disciples, and you will know the truth, and the truth will make you free." "So, if the Son makes you free, you will be free indeed." John 8:31-32, 36
- "Because the carnal mind is enmity against God: for it is not subject to the law of God, neither indeed can be. So, then they that are in the flesh cannot please God. But ye are not in the flesh, but in the Spirit, if so be that the Spirit of God dwell in you. Now if any man have not the Spirit of Christ, he is none of his." Romans 8:7-9 KJV
- "the god of this world hath blinded the minds of them which believe not, lest the light of the glorious gospel of Christ, who is the image of God, should shine unto them." 2 Corinthians 4:4 KJV

An incident in Oregon way back in '74 is worth sharing. After I told a stoned character about God's salvation & blessing, he laid some of the "evidence" above on me. He then went away "hissing & spitting" saying, "that religious rut is O.K. for you but not for me." Well, He came back several weeks later shining like a new penny with the testimony of Jesus' redeeming power. And that's my purpose writing these "G-notes." Just stir up interest in Divine things & plant a few seeds. "Taste & see that the Lord is good! Happy is the man who takes refuge in him!" Psalm 34:8 "For I know the plans I have for you, says the Lord, plans for welfare and not for evil, to give you a future and a hope. Then you will call upon me and come and pray to me, and I will hear you." Jeremiah 29:11-12 Choose Jesus, He is Alive. See also note 9 "Serving God".

138

THIS HARD WORLD

Not many would dispute the title of this G-note. Having to work to survive, deal with obstacles, physical problems, mental problems, emotional problems, and the aging process can be a constant grind. For the vast majority of folks, "This Hard World" is just reality. And I see so many folks who have one crisis after the other. My deceased sister had 9 marriages which failed in sequence, man #10 didn't marry her, but he did bury her (a distasteful rhyme there). At any rate, the Scripture does admit that this world is abrasive to humans. "Man is born to trouble as the sparks fly upward." Job 5:7 So, does Scripture offer a better plan for folks to deal with "This Hard World"??

Of course, it does. From cover to cover there are teachings that offer a better approach to living & avoiding excess problems. Long ago I personally asked, "why such a hard world?", & decided to give the Christian life a shot to see if there was anything to it. Actually, I was surprised to find the following:

- That dreaded salvation experience is not just a religious formality with lots of people looking on but can be a spiritual rebirth or awakening.
- Prayer is not a mind–numbing & empty ritual, but a connection with a higher power that sympathizes with our needs AND is willing and able to supply them. (See "What Is Prayer" note 37)
- The Bible is not boring, it is a penetrating & amazing presentation of the mind & perspectives of the living God. (See "Why The Bible" note 65)
- The minister/priest is not a "jerk w/o work." He is usually a professional who is skilled in dealing with human issues & problems. Many are trained counselors with years of experience.
- The church is not a haven of losers, but a hospital for sin sick humanity. I've found lots of quality folks there. (Occasionally a false Christian, but that's not God's fault . . .)
- Giving or tithing is not a matter of throwing money down a rat hole, but a matter of experiencing the sowing & reaping laws of God. And those laws are amazing to behold – they become part of worship at a deeper level. (See "Christian Giving" note 30)
- Faith is not for ignorant folks, but a dimension of God that opens to us

as we interact with it. Faith is not a blind leap in the dark either. It's just a matter of seeking God. (See "Faith" note 75)
- Divine Guidance is real, if we are looking for it. (See note 143.)

Well "This Hard World" keeps rolling along in space. And people keep rolling along with hard problems. Universities keep presenting Bible denying & Christ rejecting philosophies/answers for life. So, natural barriers between man & God continue to block folks from the good stuff listed above. "My people have committed two evils: they have forsaken me, the fountain of living waters, and hewed out cisterns for themselves, broken cisterns, that can hold no water." Jeremiah 2:13 Why not look to that Higher Power for some answers? Jesus Christ is notorious for infusing discipline, order, direction, & progress into the life of "whosoever" will look beyond "This Hard World" & it's hopelessness. Here are some clear teachings/promises from the Bible:

- "Thou dost show me the path of life; in thy presence there is fullness of joy, in thy right hand are pleasures for evermore." Psalms 16:11
- "O taste and see that the Lord is good: blessed is the man that trusteth in Him." Psalms 34:8 KJV
- "Take delight in the Lord, and He will give you the desires of your heart." Psalms 37:4
- "Jesus said unto them, "I am the bread of life; he that cometh to me shall never hunger; and he that believeth on me shall never thirst." John 6:35 KJV
- "Hitherto you have asked nothing in my name: ask, and you will receive, that your joy may be full. John 16:24 Jesus said that.

Those references are from the Book of Psalms and the Gospel of John. A seeker of truth & hope could gain penetrating info from just those two books of the Bible. But there's tons more "Invisible Support" (note 159) in the rest of the Book. Of course, we still have the church, & "Divine Presence," and other goodies from above which removes many of the biting teeth from "This Hard World." Choose Jesus & His value system, they are Alive. See also "Comfort From Above" note 136.

139

THE SALES PITCH*

In the last 50 years or so I have bought & sold a lot of things – cars, boats, campers, art, real estate, etc. But it's a sure thing I am not a salesman. The only sale I made as an "official salesman" was a vacuum cleaner, & that single transaction was cancelled by the customer the next day. I couldn't sell ice water to citizens of hell. And a pet peeve of mine is the street salesman (person). One desperate looking lady selling post cards in Shanghai put the cards in my hands. I gave them back to her; then she threw them at me! I could mention the timeshare sales pitch where a team of high pressure & SMART salesmen play with their subject's minds & have numerous answers for your every objection, & then say things like "what is holding you back?" Here's a few tips for dealing with the rank & intrusive sales pitch:

-terminate the salesperson (not legal, proper or righteous)	-cuff & gag him (or her)
-sit & cry like Stan Laurel (if you are an actor)	-tell them "you are ruining my day . . ." then pass out.
-run & hide	-cave in & buy the product

So, is the preacher a salesman? Or is he just blowing out "much ado about nothing." I will admit the minister, priest, evangelist is dealing with an abstract product – it can't be titled, measured, held, felt, etc., & Jesus basically left this planet 2K years ago . . . But I believe in this "product" & could "sell" Jesus. I would pay to do it (which is the case – time, computer & printer maintenance, paper, internet fees, etc.)

>> This is why "buying" Jesus is such a good DEAL:

- Jesus Christ is Deity & has Divine prerogatives: Omnipresence, Power to forgive sins, Power to raise the dead, Judge of man's eternal destiny. (see "Was Jesus God" note 97)
- Jesus is the only one that can & does see various evil contortions coming at us and shields us from them BEFORE we know they're coming. This is a nugget of truth associated with His Omniscience (& love). He can violate the laws of TIME because He invented those laws. (John 1:1-3, Colossians 1:15-20)

- Jesus Christ is the only one who has deliverance power available to get rid of clinging monkeys. Not Buddha, Mohammed, Gandhi, Joseph Smith, etc. who are all still rotting in their (holy?) graves . . . It is no secret that drugs, booze, laziness, & various kinds of craziness can & will depart from us as we realize just WHO we are walking with and draw on His power. ("Invisible Support" note 159) "But to all who received him, who believed in his name, he gave power to become children of God." John 1:12
- Jesus is that personal friend of Proverbs 18:24 "There are friends . . . but there is a friend who sticks closer than a brother." An old divine said this, "He who has Christ as a friend has an All Mighty friend." J. C. Ryle And that Robin Williams voiced genie in the cartoon classic "Aladdin" said, "You ain't never had a friend like ME!" Well, Jesus is better, and He is real.
- And Prayer is an intense benefit of walking with Jesus Christ. I believe new Christians have a special priority with God & get MORE answers & goodies more quickly than average believers. (See "What is Prayer" note 37.)
- Jesus is the "Shepherd" of Psalm 23 "The Lord is my shepherd; I shall not want . . ." Everybody knows that passage, but not this one: "The Lord is good to those who wait for him, to the soul that seeks him. It is good that one should wait quietly for the salvation of the Lord. It is good for a man that he bear the yoke in his youth." Lamentations 3:25-27

Well, there's a lot of raunchy "sales pitches" around, but the sales pitch for "buying" Jesus & His Way is not only legitimate & Biblical, it's also the best "merchandise". AND as touching the "abstract product" that can't be titled, measured, held & felt, etc, actually in the parameters of FAITH & SPIRITUALITY, all those things are possible. And we do have the written Word, which is not abstract at all, it's just a very special Book loaded with interesting stuff. "These are written that you may believe that Jesus is the Christ, the Son of God, and that believing you may have life in his name." John 20:30 "Behold, I stand at the door and knock; if any one hears my voice and opens the door, I will come in to him and eat with him, and he with me." Revelation 3:20 The resurrected Jesus Christ said that. Choose Jesus & His Word, they are Alive. See also "Concerning Resale" note 89.

* This G-note analogy may be a little controversial, and my critics may think I'm off a bit too, but you can't please all the people all the time.

140

TROUBLESOME BODY PARTS

Humans have a reputation of being troubled creatures, so it's not surprising if we have "troublesome body parts", such as:

- the brain – leads oneself astray from truth & God with false theories on many subjects
- the eyes – lust is just for starters
- the ears – selective hearing is common enough
- the tongue – this thing is maybe the worst . . . see James 3:5-10
- the hands – stealing stuff & making obscene gestures
- the heart – "The heart is deceitful above all things, and desperately corrupt; who can understand it?"
- the stomach – sucking in too much food, & booze, etc. Jeremiah 17:9
- the genitals – I read about a doctor who fell off a ladder & bashed his head. He said he left his body & experienced a realm like heaven. For some reason he reached down & checked his groin to find nothing there. My conclusion is: heaven will have no sexual temptations from either male or female desires – what a different world. . .
- the legs – run from work, church, responsibility, etc.
- the feet – "His strong steps are shortened, and his own schemes throw him down. For he is cast into a net by his own feet," Job 18:7-8

Now everyone knows that Christ had a body, and that He died, then went to heaven. Almost everyone knows that fifty days later the Holy Spirit came down & empowered believers in order to start the Christian Church. And according to Scripture the Church is the body of Christ. Ephesians 1:22-23, et al. So does the "body of Christ" have any "troublesome parts"? What about the hypocrite? The gossip artist? The occasional addict? The false minister? The obligated attendee? The family abuser? Any minister or priest will admit that not all the folks in the church are totally righteous or involved for spiritual reasons. We don't live in a perfect world. . . And the body of Christ on this planet is not perfect either.

The imperfection of the church, i.e. "Troublesome Body Parts" is fairly well known. And there are people who have been burned in church by folks who were either false Christians or just too shallow. I've met the burned – they have strong feelings <u>against</u> the church & state that "<u>all Christians</u> are false." Then there are honest folks who say they don't want to be in church because <u>they</u> will spoil the soup (be a troublesome part). I believe that using those excuses is clearly a case of <u>the brain</u> leading oneself astray.

The church is known to be a hospital for sin sick humanity. If anyone admits they have "troublesome" issues, they should go to a place that is <u>proven to be helpful</u>, NOT bash it with unreasonable arguments. Then if those same folks care about their soul, and it's eternal destiny, the Christian church is the place to be. Sure, it's not perfect, but there are a lot of good things there. I believe God is watching all of us & expecting such things as commitment to His cause. And what if there is a Divine Blessing for those who go out of their way to accept Christ & His church??

- Psalms 5:12 "For thou dost bless the righteous, O Lord; thou dost cover him with favor as with a shield."
- Lamentations 3:25 "The Lord is good to those who wait for him, to the soul that seeks him."
- John 12:26 "If anyone serves me, he must follow me; and where I am; there shall my servant be also; if anyone serves me, the Father will honor him." Jesus said that.
- 1 John 1:7 "but if we walk in the light, as he is in the light, we have fellowship with one another, and the blood of Jesus his Son cleanses us from all sin."

We will have to go out of this world to find perfection, but if we Choose Jesus and His Church, they will be found to be <u>Alive</u>. See also note 49 "Which Church Is Right?"

141

CONDENSED LABOR

Any economist should know what "Condensed Labor" is. For the rest of us it's not a well-known concept. Simply put, C.L. is money. To get money we usually work for it, and the paycheck or money we receive for that work is actually "condensed labor". That C.L. in a real sense is our life because it takes time & sweat, tears, etc. to exchange for the green stuff. It can honestly be said that young folks (or anyone) who wastes their money are wasting their life. It's sad to see the carnie or young soldier throw money from their hand as soon as they get it. They should put it in land, building, tools & equipment, transportation, etc. (capitol assets), especially in a free country, because that is a basic meaning of freedom. Of course, some hard-earned money/C.L. should go in the BANK.

Now if God is the creator, (not a big bang or evolution process) then according to the first pages of the Bible we see six days of creation (labor), then a day of rest. According to Scripture God is a person, so what would be His paycheck? It would be hard to hand the creator of life & the earth, & the universe a big bag of money. We have to figure that He just holds title to all that is seen with the human eye. The stars & sky at night, then all forms of plant & animal & marine life in daytime. It's all His:

- Job 41:11 "Who has given to me, that I should repay him? Whatever is under the whole heaven is mine."
- Psalms 50:10-12 "For every beast of the forest is mine, the cattle on a thousand hills. I know all the birds of the air, and all that moves in the field is mine. If I were hungry, I would not tell you; for the world and all that is in it is mine."
- Ezekiel 18:4 "Behold, all souls are mine; the soul of the father as well as the soul of the son is mine: the soul that sins shall die."

But what would God's "money" be if we could reduce it all down to the basics? I believe YOU should look in the mirror. That human looking back at you is the highest form of all creation, and the reason it was all created. Look at Genesis 1:26-30. People are God's "money". This analogy makes more sense when we look at the Incarnation of Christ, and consider that He came here (at great labor & cost, see note 7) to redeem us from sin, so we can be put in the eternal BANK – heaven. "God so loved the world that he gave his only Son, that whoever believes in him should not perish but have eternal life." John 3:16 I suppose God also invests in capital assets – land, buildings, equipment, etc. That would be the physical church buildings, church schools & hospitals around the world, etc. But the "money", or best "condensed labor" is people – SOULS.

The appeal of this Gospel-note is just this. Are you blocking God from putting His hard earned "money" in the "BANK"?? Is your pride, ego, intellect, etc. holding you back from accepting Christ & that salvation package? If so, you not only frustrate a hard working Creator & steal His "money", but you also cheat your own self out of Divine blessings here on planet earth, AND your share of what that "bank" in the sky is all about. For a glimpse of it see John 14:1-7 and Revelation 21:1-5. The Bible is AWESOME for showing these truths, and tons of others. . . Choose Jesus, He is Alive. See also note 125, "Only God Could Make".

142

GOD'S NOT DEAD

We recently watched the Philosophical movie of the above title. It depicts a young man in a typical state university taking a required philosophy class where the professor was extremely atheist & determined to show his class that God IS dead. The young Christian man takes the Profs. challenge to show the evidence that Profs. position is wrong. Well it was a very interesting & penetrating movie, maybe a little dramatized for effect. But I got an EXTRA kick from this movie because 40 years ago I was in nearly the same situation in real life. Only the philosophy professor was my boss.

Jeff M. (assumed name) was an active duty Army Chaplain of United Methodist background. I was the Chap. Assistant. We were in an isolated Hawk missile battalion in Key West, Florida. Since he had a master's degree also in Philo., he was paid by the local college to teach the Philo. class to soldiers needing that class. I studied the required books & positions of philosophy & wrote a paper or two. But even though I was a new Christian at that time I noticed some of his extremely liberal beliefs. I asked direct (&probably blunt) questions on basic Bible doctrines which he simply didn't believe. I now know that working with him was a "Divine Appointment" for both of us. For me God intended to stimulate my thinking – for J. M. God put a saved believer under his atheist nose. Here are some of his statements that I have reflected on for the past 40 years.

- "I don't want to cut my head off." That is intellectual pride which blocks many from making a stand for the Bible & Gospel of Christ.
- "You are all O.K. as you are." We gave many soldier retreats/functions where movies, talks, testimonies, barbeques, etc. were done for morale support. His "all O.K." statements were a direct contradiction of New Testament teaching.
- "I don't disbelieve it." Philosophers typically ask questions more than holding blunt positions of unbelief on any subject.
- "I don't want to defend God." Well, that is exactly what the paid professional minister should be doing. All Christians should make a stand, but the leader especially should defend Biblical positions & truths with a passion because they ARE on a mission.
- "You are a mess Fred." and – "My retarded assistant. . ." While working w/J.M. God gave me a premium revelation of Jesus Christ, see note 7 "I

Saw The King".

- Colossians 2:8 "See to it that no one makes a prey of you by philosophy and empty deceit, according to human tradition, according to the elemental spirits of the universe, and not according to Christ."
- 2 Timothy 3:12-13 "Indeed all who desire to live a godly life in Christ Jesus will be persecuted, while evil men and <u>impostors</u> will go on from bad to worse, deceivers and deceived." See note 57 "Imposters".

The movie "God's Not Dead" depicted the philosopher & the challenger as "nose to nose" & toe to toe", but it just wasn't like that with me & my chaplain boss. We actually had a good team ministry, AND something like professional friendship. Surprisingly, he allowed me to choose many of the ministry type films we presented to soldiers (some showings over 100 in attendance.) He even allowed me to speak & give testimony of divine miracles & visions I'd had. His understanding of spirituality – we invented God – made him open to the conservative viewpoint. And I do believe he was on trial by the Holy Spirit of God, and if so, he failed, because after 2 years he did fire me. But God gave me a better assignment elsewhere. P.T.L.

Well truly "God's Not Dead". My experience before J.M. & since has been "full" of God because He <u>blesses</u> those who seek Him, <u>and we have.</u> See Lamentations 3:25-27. The Methodist church <u>has entered into decline</u> due to its liberalness, and last time I talked to J.M. he seemed cold & unfriendly, probably due to reading "Concerning Quicksand", note 17 one of my earliest Gospel-notes dealing with rank unbelief.

My conclusion is this. Biblical Faith & seeking God has its rewards. My last 45 years have been a blessed adventure. The philosophy crowd & liberals work hard to deny God & Christianity and appear to be lost & without God's blessing. It's easy to avoid that hopelessness – Choose Jesus, He is Alive. Avoid hell at all costs – I've heard it will be hot down there . . . See also "Waxing Philosophical" note 67.

143

DIVINE GUIDANCE

With the premise that God is Alive, and that He is good natured, and that He gives good stuff to His own, tapping into D.G. could only be a good thing. From the start of my Christian experience in '72, D.G. seemed natural, & it paid off quite well. I got lost on Ft. Carson, CO in a snow, & said "Lord, show me where to go." Turn right, turn left, go straight, right in there; seemed to echo in my mind. Through that D.G. I met my excellent wife of 46 yrs. My son has a similar story of getting lost in Japan – just no female prize for him.

"Divine Guidance" is a benefit of FAITH. Sometimes there's guidance even before we ask. I believe the key to this is WANTING D.G. – it honors the Holy Spirit & it's a clean heart attitude. We have found that MUCH D.G. just happens – doors shut & doors open on their own, things just "click" so well, God is obviously involved. This is an awesome benefit of walking with Jesus Christ.

Now much of D.G. is from the Word. We heard recently, "God never stops talking to us till we close the Book." Bob Riggs (assumed name). This means familiarity with Scripture produces MUCH guidance. The general content & principles of the Book are loaded w/clear examples on many subjects: Genesis stories contain interesting perspective on God's early dealings. Proverbs for practical tips galore. The teachings of Christ are rich with guiding principles. Then one could ask, "What would Jesus do in this situation?" Well, if we aren't even spending time in the gospels of Matt., Mark, Luke, & John; we might not know what He would do. Then the epistles of the Apostles & Paul are excellent & touch many subjects. Shame on the Christian who neglects the Word . . . It's so dynamic & Alive & a part of the victory in Christ, (not just on the subject of D.G.). "Faith comes by hearing, and hearing by the word of God." Romans 10:17

In a general sense, D.G. is a primary principle of the Bible. There is a premium account of D.G. in Acts 8:26-35 where Phillip was told by an angel to go to the Ethiopian eunuch of the queen & explain what he was reading from the scroll of Isaiah. The Holy Spirit also "spoke" to Phillip. Now today Divine Guidance seems to be more subtle. It might be the still, small "voice" of our conscience echoing in our mind. Maybe God will send someone, or some situation that sheds light specifically on our direction question. Maybe a book will "fall" into our hands. Intuition may dawn in an unusually strong manner on the subject. And I personally wouldn't rule out dreams & visions – God has given me some very clear guidance this way. See Joel 2:28

But what to do when we are "read-up", "prayed-up", & wanting D.G., & NOTHING is clear on an issue where we need direction. We can be sure God will lead, but the Divine answer may be "wait". And humans usually want things now or yesterday. Patience can be in short supply. We have used a "fleece" at times (see Judges 6:36-40) – maybe tossing a coin after praying for direction. (Once we tossed it 2 times & took 2 out of two heads to mean "yes".) Other times NOTHING was clear & we figured it was a NO. Of course, Scripture has something to say on this subject:

- "Thou dost guide me with thy counsel, and afterward thou wilt receive me to glory." Psalms 73:24
- "Trust in the Lord with all thine heart and lean not on thine own understanding. In all thy ways acknowledge him, and he shall direct thy paths." Proverbs 3:5-6
- "The path of the righteous is like the light of dawn, which shines brighter and brighter until full day." Proverbs 4:18
- "the Lord will guide you continually, and satisfy your desire with good things, and make your bones strong. . ." Isaiah 58:11a

The concept of Divine Guidance is found in the Book from cover to cover. And it's a totally valid benefit or principle of the Christian faith experience. It can be a valuable asset to the saved individual, but w/o salvation it's usually considered to be rubbish, or a silly myth. Choose Jesus, He is Alive. And realize that Divine Guidance (and lots of other goodies from above), are waiting to be "picked". See also note 28 "What's in It For Me".

144

LAME THINKING

In the world that we all live in there is a lot of good thinking. Early on man invented the wheel. About that time, he learned to cook his food for better taste & to kill germs, etc. He learned to ride a mule or horse to save wear & tear on his own legs. There has been lots of good thinking in man's history, & the U.S. constitution & free enterprise principles are most brilliant, but here are some lame strokes:

- Predicting rain in AZ is usually lame thinking . . .
- It's lame to believe you can become an astronaut because one such character said you could do/be "anything you want." While optimism & encouragement is good, we all have limits–only God is unlimited . . .
- It's lame to think all folks of one ethnic group are bad because one in particular appears to be.
- "Putting a computer chip in all things is the way to go." That's pure lame thinking – some things are best left alone. In Japan they have even computerized the toilet seat & have a console beside it.
- How about the man who gets in a sleeping bag with 24 live rattlesnakes? Wouldn't <u>that</u> be "lame thinking?" See note 61 "Obsessions."
- Judging a book (or person) by its cover is classic L.T., but all too common.
- It's lame thinking for a young preacher to bash the work of an older one, not knowing (or caring) where & what the older one has seen & been through. See note 52 "The Game."
- Having numerous degrees makes one more capable of good thinking. This may be true, <u>but</u> why did the most educated of the nation of Israel condemn Christ to death, when they KNEW He had replaced blind eyes, walked on water, <u>raised the dead</u>, etc.?? Lame thinking by committee.
- To put the care of one's eternal soul in the hands of atheists such as C. Darwin & Steve Hawking is lame thinking. Heaven is too long & hell is too hot to accept their anti-Christ, (anti Bible, anti-Creation, anti-Gospel, etc.), thinking without studying the Book carefully for oneself.
- Considering Jesus Christ to be just "an iconic character" is close to lame thinking. Jesus is either God in the flesh as he claimed (John 14:7-9) or he was a lunatic – God didn't give any middle ground on this . . .

Well it's a sure thing I have done my share of L.T. in my days. But at the age of 20 I made a resolution to study the Book thoroughly to see if it was really special or "Holy" as such. I knew it was often used as a door stop or placed in the back of some cabinet or closet. It seemed to deserve better if God prepared it (which 2 Timothy 3:16, Hebrews 4:12 clearly states.) If the world is so loaded with L.T., maybe God's book would reveal some good thinking. Good thinking was only the beginning. I also found a goldmine of history, drama, man reasoning w/God, God reasoning w/man (Genesis 18:22-33, Job 40 &41), good & bad character traits, God's humor in the miraculous, the justice & judgment of God, the reason for life (Acts 17:26), then God revealed as a man in Jesus Christ. Nothing could be more amazing in a world full of "lame thinking."

Here's a few "thoughts from above" which may fit this essay:

- Psalms 1:1 "Blessed is the man that walketh not in the counsel of the ungodly, nor standeth in the way of sinners, nor sitteth in the seat of the scornful." KJV (All of Psalms 1 is Bible Truth 101).
- Jeremiah 2:13 "for my people have committed two evils: they have forsaken me the fountain of living waters, and hewed out cisterns for themselves, broken cisterns, that can hold no water." (the root of Lame Thinking)
- Mark 8:38 "For whoever is ashamed of me and of my words in this adulterous and sinful generation, of him will the Son of man also be ashamed, . . ." Jesus said that.
- Romans 1:28 "And since they did not see fit to acknowledge God, God gave them up to a base mind and to improper conduct." (Today's liberals & academia? ?)
- 2 Corinthians 11:3 "I am afraid that as the serpent deceived Eve by his cunning, your thoughts will be led astray from a sincere and pure devotion to Christ."
- 2 John 9 "Whoever goes ahead and does not abide in the doctrine of Christ does not have God; he who abides in the doctrine of Christ has both the Father and the Son."

I know people think & believe whatever they want, but it would seem best to minimize "lame thinking." Maximize the good stuff & be blessed, for time AND eternity. "Behold, I stand at the door and knock; if anyone hears my voice and opens the door, I will come in to him and eat with him, and he with me." Revelation 3:20 Choose Jesus, He is Alive. See also "Was Jesus God?" note 97.

145

WHAT'S IN THE HOUSE?

There appears to be lots of things in the typical house/home. You will have furniture & appliances, beds, TV/stereo, clothing, wall pictures, house plants, dogs, cats, mice, & maybe a few bugs. (Possibly a certain amount of dirt & slime & debris for messy folks.) But are there unseen elements?

Jesus Christ dealt with unseen entities all the time in the 4 gospels – mostly demons. Today they still exist, and often create bizarre behavior as they did then, 2,000 years ago. I believe that behavior today is different in manifestation to fit modern times & thought. Besides promoting the works of the flesh mentioned by Paul the Apostle – ". . . sorcery, hatred, quarreling, jealousy, anger, selfishness, slander . . .," demons also promote incest & gender confusion. Now less than 2% of gender confusion is physical, "ambiguous genitalia" according to medical books. The vast majority is a mental "disorientation" & I believe mostly demon influenced. How could the god of this world & spiritual adversary of humans more effectively foul the fabric of society than by tampering with God given gender assignments??

Other problems in the house from negative spiritual influence would be excessive sickness (see Psalm 91), drug & alcohol abuse/habits, general bad luck, and even our animals can be affected – often pets can reflect the evil spirit/attitude of the folks they are close to. However, demons can be friendly fellows as long as there is no inclination towards Jesus Christ & His church & value system. From a Biblical point of view, if we allow these evil entities to dwell with us, it cannot bode well for our home OR our eternal souls . . . And I know this material may be offensive, but it does square with my past 47 years Christian study & experience, with what I see now, and Scripture teaching. I also know the atheist mind says all this is bunk, BUT they say all creation & life forms happened by chance, which is much harder to believe.

Probably a strong reason I fear our homes can have uninvited entities is an experience of mine in the fall of '69 in a California dorm room – see note 34 "The Demon". I "saw" that character, & he wasn't offering hope or truth, to say the least . . . I wasn't close to, or seeking God which is why he came in. They say "nature abhors a vacuum," well w/o welcoming the Biblical God in our dwellings, we can expect un-holy entities. For the sake of contrast in this essay, The Blessing of God is what folks should want for their house/home. See Psalm 128 for a brief summary. Long before David's time the Blessing is mentioned by Moses:

- Genesis 39:5 ". . . the blessing of the Lord was upon all that he had, in house and field."
- Deuteronomy 28:6 "Blessed shall you be when you come in and blessed shall you be when you go out."
- Zachariah 5:1-4 "This is the curse . . . and it shall enter the house of the thief, and the house of him who swears falsely by my name; and it shall abide in his house and consume it . . ." (The flying scroll is in a spiritual dimension. It's 10 by 20 cubits, about 15 -30 ft & hovers over lost folk's houses like the "sword of Damocles".) What is written on it? See also Proverbs 3:33.
- Isaiah 13:21 "But wild beasts of the desert shall lie there; and their houses shall be full of doleful creatures; and owls shall dwell there, and satyrs shall dance there." (Beautiful symbolism, and this may also speak of the condition of the US after it falls completely to godless liberalism.)
- Mark 3:25 "if a house is divided against itself, that house will not be able to stand." (Words of Christ)
- James 4:7-8 "Submit yourselves therefore to God. Resist the devil and he will flee from you. Draw near to God and he will draw near to you. . ."
- Revelation 3:20 "Behold, I stand at the door and knock; if anyone hears my voice and opens the door, I will come in to him and eat with him, and he with me." (The resurrected Jesus Christ said that.)

Choose Jesus & His Spirit, they are Alive, and are much better house guests. See also note 66 "The Blessing & the Curse".

146

NOTORIOUS STATEMENTS

People have been making "Notorious Statements" from the beginning of time. In the last 100 years or so with ambitious journalists & writers & recording devices, it's best to say little – or – "think twice & say nothing" anon., or you may be quoted. Some "notorious statements" may be good for humor but lack character & truth. Here's a few – from prominent sources:

- Tom Brokaw, Am. journalist "We don't just have egg on our face. We have omelet all over our suits."
- Don Marquis, Am. poet & journalist "an optimist is a guy that has never had much experience."
- Winston Churchill, "I am fond of pigs. Dogs look up to us. Cats look down on us. Pigs treat us as equals."
- Richard Nixon, "People have got to know whether or not their President is a crook. Well, I'm not a crook."
- Dean Martin, Am. singer "You are not drunk if you can lie on the floor without holding on."

— More Serious Clips —

- John Maynard Keynes, English economist, "In the long run, we are all dead."
- Albert Einstein, "God is subtle, but He is not malicious . . . I am convinced that He does not play dice." (Did Albert have a couple Baptist bones with that suggestion of predestination/election??)
- G.K. Chesterton, English novelist, "The Christian ideal has not been tried and found wanting. It has been found difficult; and left untried. . . when men stop believing in God, they don't believe in nothing; they believe in anything."
- Adolf Hitler, Lucifer incarnate from 1920-45?? "The broad mass of a nation . . . will more easily fall victim to a big lie, than to a small one." (A couple big lies in our day appears to be atheism & political correctness, promoted by academia & the liberal left.)
- Steve Hawking, English theoretical physicist, cosmologist, "If we find the answer to that (why it is that WE and the universe exist), it would be the ultimate triumph of human reason – for then we would know the mind of God."

Well I would suspect that Steve Hawking never tried the Christian ideal – the Word of God – for truth & answers. Acts 17:26-27 Clearly gives the purpose of life; "He made from one every nation of men to live on all the face of the earth, having determined allotted periods and the boundaries of their habitation, that they should seek God, in the hope that they might feel after him and find him." Millions of Christians of all ages & denominations will identify with that reference. And my own "notorious statement" is this; "God is alive and will reveal Himself, if we honor Jesus Christ and His Word." But today's trend towards atheism & political correctness (especially at the universities) has rule #1 – no God, WE don't go there.

Now a character named Pilate had the actual Jesus Christ before himself for judgment & asked Jesus "What is truth?" Is it any surprise that after asking that question, Pilate had Truth Incarnate executed? Is that what atheists & agnostics today are doing?? Assassinating TRUTH?? I know people today could find truth in the Word if they really wanted it. But in the air around us is a spirit that prefers "the lie." That spirit promotes falseness & sets folks up to lose in the truth arena. 2 Corinthians 4:4 "The god of this world has blinded the minds of the unbelievers, to keep them from seeing the light of the gospel of the glory of Christ, . . ."

Salman Rushdie, (British-Indian novelist) high on Islam's hit list, had this to say, "One of the things a writer is for is to say the unsayable, speak the unspeakable, and ask difficult questions." (Gospel Notes??) People should know that Scripture has a lot of serious "notorious statements", and MANY of those writers were executed by the spirit of the world, or those controlled by it. Maybe the most penetrating (and notorious) statement was made by Jesus Christ himself. John 14:6 "I am the way, and the truth, and the life. No one comes to the Father, except through me." If Jesus was stating TRUTH, then that truth holds today. So, are YOU saved by Jesus Christ and moving towards God?? Or are you listening to silly notorious statements like this, "heaven doesn't want me, and hell is afraid I'll take over."?? Try Jesus and His Word, they are Alive. Connect with a legitimate Bible teaching group & support it. And look forward to hearing the most excellent "Notorious Statement" of all Matthew 25:21 "Well done, good and faithful servant, you have been faithful over a little, I will set you over much; enter into the joy of your master." See also "Famous Last Words" note 58.

147

THE NATURE OF GOD

What is God like? is a HUGE question for humans, and it should be addressed by a team of doctorate level theologians. However, lots of diversity, tradition, & philosophy rambling would only confuse the matter. Most preachers would simply present God's attributes such as holiness, eternity, life, immutability, omnipotence, omniscience, author of salvation, forgiveness, receives prayer & worship, then of course judgment. But all of that would be out of the scope of this short essay. This Gospel-note considers "the Nature of God" from what is revealed about God in the Bible. And God's source book alone speaks loudly of His character/nature.

- "*God created man in his own image; in the image of God he created him; male and female he created them.*" Genesis 1:27 Creation is mentioned three times here - and throughout the Book creation is a constant theme. God's nature is to make things out of nothing - class act?? No human can do that.
- "*The Lord sees not as man sees; man looks on the outward appearance, but the Lord looks on the heart.*" 1 Samuel 16:7b Almost like God has X-ray vision. We see the surface - He sees in depth.
- "*the ravens brought him bread and meat in the morning and bread and meat in the evening . . .*" Kings 17:6 This little known & simple MIRACLE speaks of God's sense of humor. But Scripture has loads of AWESOME miracles to challenge the pride & ego of intellectual man. Much of God's nature & character is seen in the MAGNITUDE of Biblical miracles. And they still happen today. See "My Miracles" note 33.
- God as a man of war - Exodus 14-15 Scripture reveals the aggressive side of God's nature very boldly in this Exodus event in Moses' time. Also, many other events in the Old Testament are striking. And the concept of end times great tribulation & judgement of the whole world is VERY Biblical, and just a part of God's nature.
- "*Look among the nations and see; wonder and be astounded. For I am doing a work in your days that you would not believe if told.*" Habakkuk 1:5 In that day 650 years B.C. the Chaldeans were to punish Israel for its sin, which happened. Then Messiah/Christ came at the appointed time to be the lamb of God for sin. People who think are overwhelmed at the notion that God would appear as a baby, born in an animal

shelter, claim to be God (John 14:9) & do miracles & boldly DIE for our sin. God's nature of LOVE shines through here . . . (The question now is, what kind of amazing thing will God do in our day??)

- "Jesus declared, *I thank thee Father, Lord of heaven and earth, that thou hast hidden these things from the wise and understanding and revealed them to babes . . .*" Matthew 11:25-26 Blocking Divine truth from the proud & successful and revealing it to the humble is a powerful picture of God's nature. And Jesus Christ chose disciples from common stock. The Apostle Paul was a different bird with degrees untold, but God had to knock him silly to see the light – Acts 9.
- "*the Word of God is living and active, sharper than any two-edged sword . . . before him no creature is hidden . . .*" Hebrews 4:12 This reference speaks of the Scripture AND Christ. A mystical union that baffles all theologians to pieces. The book of Scripture itself is unlike any other book. But blend it with Jesus Christ as God's VOICE today and you have an awesome combo. Only the nature & character of God could have produced this mystical union of the written Word & Jesus Christ Himself.
- "*Eye has not seen, nor ear heard, nor have entered into the heart of man, the things which God has prepared for those who love Him.*" 1 Corinthians 2:9 This is commonly taken as a reference to Heaven & eternal life. It may also refer to spiritual goodies in this life (Isaiah64:4, Ephesians 2:4-7), but Jesus did refer to heaven often. And providing a heaven for the redeemed is a premium illustration of God's character & LOVE. His JUSTICE is seen in providing a hell for those who reject their creator & Biblical salvation, then live a life of sin & self . . .

Untouchable questions such as: how old is God?, where did He come from?, where is His throne?, etc. may be moot issues. But it IS God's nature to reveal Himself through faith, & in the Bible, & bless those who seek Him. If we toss the Book (or undermine its authority), we lose the best source of info on God's nature. Then we may end up with some odd form of false God, or no God, & that will be an eternal disaster. Why take that chance?? Hell already has enough citizens . . . Choose Jesus & His Word, they are Alive, and really do reveal "The Nature of God". See also "Was Jesus God?" note 97.

148

STAIRCASE TO HEAVEN

In This life there appears to be a "highway" to hell, and a "Staircase to Heaven". Recently some rock music groups have titled two songs this way. I suppose the highway to hell is easier & appeals to more folks. BUT the "Staircase to Heaven" is there too, just more difficult & not as well traveled.

Now the SPIRAL stair to me is a likely symbol of the Staircase to Heaven because even the upward path of God is not straight & direct – it's a curving challenge & meant to be. I'm told the medieval castle spiral stair goes up and to the right (or clockwise) & is designed that way so castle defenders coming down have a right-handed advantage to swing swords. But Christ & angels defend God's "castle" & upward path and they are in business to HELP the seeker of Truth rather than hinder. Ref. Hebrews 1:14 The hindrances will come from our selves & fellow humans.

One "curve" we meet on the "Staircase to Heaven" is persecution outside the church, and then shallow Christians in the Church, who do things in the religious group that muddies the "water" & ruins new believers. Unnecessary "stuff" like cold shoulder, petty judgment, subtle games, etc. against the Spirit of fellowship. Jesus & the Apostles said, "Love one another", but pursuers of God will be occasionally met by falseness in the church – see "The Game" note 52 or "Imposters" note 57. Often when we get our eyes off Jesus Christ, we can easily lose our footing. And of course, our spiritual adversary is very capable & will always trip us & spoil our progress upwards. See Ephesians 6.

A hobby of mine is to make welded spirals – five of them so far. The spiral I want to build next goes around twice, (did it, Sep.'17) but God's spiral S.T.H. just keeps going round & round all the way up, and it can be wearisome. Sometimes landings seem to happen where we are stuck for a while – maybe for rest. Psalm 23:1-2 "The Lord is my shepherd; I shall not want; he makes me lie down in green pastures. He leads me beside still waters; he restores my soul."

In spite of the problems of the "Staircase to Heaven" & step-by-step journey upwards, it's worth it because if you deal with the challenges you will see Jesus & your purpose of life more clearly. "The path of the righteous is like the light of dawn, which shines brighter and brighter until full day." Proverbs 4:18 That reference goes on in verse 19 to clearly show the other side of the coin – those folks who ditch the S.T.H. and go the other way. "The way of the wicked is like deep darkness; they do not know over what they stumble." For a misguided word "picture" of that other path today, Google the lyrics of AC-DC "Highway to Hell".

- Psalms 37:23-24 "The steps of a man are from the Lord, and he establishes him in whose way he delights; though he fall, he shall not be cast headlong, for the Lord is the stay of his hand.
- Habakkuk 3:19* KJV "The Lord God is my strength, and he will make my feet like hinds' feet, and he will make me to walk upon mine high places. . ."
- Matthew 7:13-14 "Enter by the narrow gate; for the gate is wide and the way is easy, that leads to destruction, and those who enter by it are many. For the gate is narrow and the way is hard, that leads to life, and those who find it are few." Jesus said that.
- Philippians 4:13 KJV "I can do all things through Christ which strengtheneth me."
- 1 Peter 4:12 "Beloved, do not be surprised at the fiery ordeal which comes upon you to prove you, as though something strange were happening to you."

Well, I'm convinced it's better to "spiral" up & be blessed, than to Highway down towards the undesirable place. I've heard it's hot down there – The Lord said it was. See "I Saw the King" note 7. Try Jesus, He is Alive.

149

THE RADIAL ENGINE

In High School I studied aircraft engines as an elective class, then a little more after H.S. in an A & P school in Englewood Calif. The Army had fixed wing cargo planes w/radial engines during the Viet Nam campaign. The "radial" is actually quite antique in design, but amazing in many ways. It has an ODD number of cylinders with the top being the "master" cylinder. The remaining cylinders – 4, 6, or 8 of them are placed around the circular design for maximum cooling airflow. Inside you have a crankshaft with only <u>one</u> throw. The master rod serves the master cylinder, then the rest of the rods (articulating) connect around the base of the master rod. Since all the rods connect to the master, there is more <u>heat</u> in the master cylinder. Now the radial engine is a LOW SPEED engine which Christ has also been in the world. "Though the mills of God grind slowly. Yet they grind exceedingly small. Though with patience He stands waiting. With exactness grinds He all." Longfellow

Now there are some other parallels in this ANALOGY with the spiritual world. The radial engine is the power of God in action. The master rod & Cylinder is Jesus Christ. He has taken a lot of <u>heat</u> especially since being born as a man at year 1 AD, predicted 700 years earlier by Isaiah the prophet (and others); "He was wounded for our transgressions, he was bruised for our iniquities; upon him was the chastisement that made us whole, and with his stripes we are healed. All we like sheep have gone astray; we have turned everyone to his own way; and the Lord has laid on him the iniquity of us all." Isaiah 53:5-6 The <u>articulating rods & cylinders</u> are the assistants & helps such as Apostles, prophets, angels, the Word, direct miracles, etc., that all connect to the "master". All of this is enclosed by God which compares to the crankcase. Inside the crankcase the oil (the Holy Spirit), is flowing intensely to lubricate the crankshaft or action of God that pulls the aircraft through the air.

The "aircraft" is the church which transports believers in Christ from the point of evangelization & rebirth (John 3:3), to that point where they pass into God's eternal kingdom. Now of course this "aircraft" is often ignored by unsaved folks on the ground, who don't always know or care that God's church is passing "over" or by. It's sad because in a legitimate church you have a Salvation factor which brings much good & blessing even to this temporary earth life. See "What's in It For Me?" note 28. For those who hear the "aircraft" & it's "engine", they can freely climb aboard & "fly" with confidence.

- Isaiah 40:31 "but they who wait for the Lord shall renew their strength, they shall mount up with wings like eagles, they shall run and not be weary, they shall walk and not faint."
- John 6:37 "All that the Father gives me will come to me; and him who comes to me I will not cast out."
- Romans 3:23-24 "since all have sinned and fall short of the glory of God, they are justified by his grace as a gift, through the redemption which is in Christ Jesus."
- Colossians 2:9-10, 12 "For in him the whole fullness of deity dwells bodily, and you have come to fullness of life in him, who is the head of all rule and authority. . . and you were buried with him in baptism, in which you were also raised with him through faith in the working of God, who raised him from the dead."

Choose Jesus and His Church, they are Alive. And as the Radial Engine clatters & thumps through the air, we can be included, and enjoy the adventurous ride. . . See also "The Take Off" note 22.

150

THE DANCE

This is moving the body and feet in rhythm, ordinarily to music (Webster). Of course, many animals & birds have dances. But humans also have the abstract contorted dance of daily balancing religion, politics, and class struggle. And we are all into this awkward "dance."

- Religion – all folks have their persuasion whether Catholic, Protestant, Jewish, & even atheism/liberalism can be embraced as a religion ("right or wrong, truth be damned" . . .) Anon. A brief study of the Gospels will show that Jesus Christ was careful to "dance" with all types.
- Politics – we hold our political position dearly whether we understand freedom or our political system. We are what we are: Republican, Democrat, or middle ground blokes. And we typically think all others are WRONG. How human is this?? (See "Human Nature", note 182.)
- Class Struggle – I figure in the American society there are maybe 50 economic levels commonly thought of as the Ladder of Success. At any rung of the ladder, it's typical for folks to avoid those below, and HATE or be jealous of those above. Then some people gauge their righteousness on being at the bottom of the ladder of success – many homeless people & religious orders have this mindset. Others think righteousness is being more productive & at the top rungs of the ladder. Actually, the Ladder of Success has little to do with right standing w/ God. Some thinker said this: "A man ought not to value himself by his achievements, or rare qualities of wit; much less by his riches, virtue or kindred." Anon.

Well, all contortions will be found in this unfriendly "dance" of religion, politics, & class struggle. And why do we have this dance? I believe it is due to American freedom to choose our religion, politics, and social class. Because we are free to choose, we must do that, & it can be difficult. In another land where someone else does the thinking & choosing, it would be easier to feel righteous in the arenas above.

So how does the Book offer any hope to the religious, political & class struggle "dance" of this world? Simply by revealing God's standards:

- Proverbs 22:2 "The rich and the poor meet together; the Lord is the maker of them all."
- Jeremiah 9:23 "Let not the wise man glory in his wisdom, let not

the mighty man glory in his might, let not the rich man glory in his riches; 24 but let him who glories glory in this, that he understands and knows me, that I am the Lord who practice kindness, justice, and righteousness in the earth; . . ."

- Romans 10:3 "For, being ignorant of the righteousness that comes from God, and seeking to establish their own, they did not submit to God's righteousness."
- Romans 10:4 "For Christ is the end of the law, that everyone who has faith may be justified." (That's God's righteousness.)

People should blend the resurrected/living Christ into their difficult "dance" w/religion, politics, & class struggle to make better sense of the world. And on judgment day before God, if there is a question WHY we consider ourselves righteous, we do well NOT to point at our denomination or political standing or achievements. Point only to Christ, His sacrificial "dance" – all of it - death, burial & resurrection, that's God's righteousness, if we receive it.* Choose Jesus, He is Alive. Revelation 3:20 "Behold, I stand at the door and knock; if anyone hears my voice and opens the door, I will come in to him and eat with him, and he with me."

* From "What is the Gospel" Greg Gilbert, 2010

151

DIVINE APPOINTMENTS

There are books by the above title, so I did not invent the phrase. But for years the concept has impressed my mind. Divine Appointments are situations or events that are extraordinary and seem to have more meaning or content as we look back & reflect on them. Like there was a plan greater than chance. And D.A.'s can be evil or good.

An example of an apparent evil D.A. is maybe an accident or sickness which blocks an outing. Then we learn that had we gone on the planned trip we would have died in the plane crash. Or something like pathological depression from grief that leads to seeking God for answers. "Godly grief produces a repentance that leads to salvation and brings no regret, but worldly grief produces death." 2 Corinthians 7:10 But apparent evil D.A.'s do more than bring folks to repentance & salvation – they also bring perspective & FAITH.

An example of a good D.A. is something that averts an accident or suicide. Maybe someone or something coming along at the right time with the right WORD or genuine help. I had a D.A. in Viet Nam which clearly showed the providence of God and turned out good. I had washed my hands in acid by mistake, then ran for the distant water faucet which was sometimes dry. But that time there was water AND a bar of soap waiting. Soap is exactly what I needed to neutralize the acid burn. That event spoke loudly that Someone was watching over my young life, and able to intervene. (A few other events over there, which could have been fatal were certainly good D.A.'s also). But nearly ALL Divine Appointments echo in the mind and have God's signature. And they teach us. "the anointing which you received from him abides in you, and you have no need that any one should teach you; as his anointing teaches you about everything, and is true, and is no lie, just as it has taught you, abide in him." 1 John 2:27 Of course, this ref. doesn't mean avoid the church, it means God's direct involvement or touch can give profound info to the individual.

A dramatic example of the D.A. in the Old Testament could be Daniel in the den of lions. Daniel 6:6-24 His FAITH & trust in God made ALL the difference, and he surely emerged from that D.A. with MORE faith than before – (along with the king who was duped to have Daniel thrown in there). In the New Testament we can cite the case of Paul the "to be" apostle being stricken with temporary blindness to be instructed by

God. Acts 9:1-19 And both of those characters were human like you & me.

The amazing part of the Divine Appointment is the timing. These events come without our knowledge or consent. They just happen & God's hand is more obvious as we reflect back on them. (see note 70 "The Chaplains") It's like God made the appointment for His purpose – without consulting with us; which only makes sense if He is the Big Boss, and Owner of all things. "I form light and create darkness, I make weal and create woe, I am the Lord, who do all these things." Isaiah 45:7

Look for God's hand in your life. Some people believe that Divine Appointments happen every day. And if we can see "cage rattling" & apparently evil issues as useful & meant to instruct us, we can benefit from many hardships & disasters of life. The good D.A.'s can reveal God's presence, and His character. Of course, if we are seeking God, we will naturally see more Divine Appointments in this life. And we should all keep in mind our certain & final D.A., "it is appointed for men to die once, and after that comes judgment,". Hebrews 9:27 This G-note barely scratches the surface of the Divine Appointment. For an in-depth & excellent book on the title above see Divine Appointments: Igniting Your Passion to Fulfill Your Destiny.[8] Choose Jesus, He is Alive. See also "Divine Presence" note 73.

152

SEEKING GOD

What is "Seeking God"? It could almost be an abstract kind of thing with so many religions and concepts of God in this world. Is it a "do it yourself" approach to religion, or is it just a decision to "get religion", and life answers?

Why "Seek God"? At least it's part of anyone's world view to have a concept of God & basic knowledge of a few religions. My personal reason for Seeking God was to find peace, purpose, fulfillment, etc., and I did find those things. But now I know "Seeking God" is the main reason we are on this planet. Acts 17:26 (below) reveals this to those who believe Scripture. Also, I now know God is able to BLESS people, & "Seeking God" promotes that blessing.

How can people "Seek God"? Some claim to be doing it on the golf course. Some thru drug induced meditation, or Eastern religions. Some claim to be getting inspiration as they climb mountains. But usually it's church attendance, religious music, Scripture, reading inspirational books, etc. I believe these NORMAL actions in "Seeking God" don't go far without decision, commitment, & determination towards Jesus Christ & His value system. With only half-hearted or insincere "Seeking of God", folks may easily find false religion or demons instead. If we have a sincere desire to find God, the GOSPEL and a legitimate church will somehow come to us.

So what is the GOSPEL? It's what the Apostle Peter took to Cornelius by Divine mandate in Acts chapter 10. "He (Jesus Christ) is the one ordained by God to be judge of the living and the dead. To him all the prophets bear witness that everyone who believes in him receives forgiveness of sin through his name." v. 42-43 Churches that promote this doctrine are on the right track. And there is a mysterious chemistry, or spiritual glow that some churches have, but that "magic?" comes & goes with time. Denominational vitality doesn't appear to be a constant or steady thing. (This is NOT a reference to the group we are currently attending.) We should trust God to give guidance to find the right church, but church cannot be the whole diet in "Seeking God". And the landscape is littered with discouraged believers who had a bad experience with a dead church & shallow believer - (years ago we had one of the very worst experiences, but we don't blame God for that.) See "Which Church is Right" and "The Gopher" notes 49 & 82.

I believe "Seeking God" is a two-way street where God is also moving toward the individual and stirring up interest. You might not be reading this if God hadn't given the urge to do so. He can also reveal things personally to you which is the business of revelation He's been in for thousands of years now. And Scripture is PURE revelation:

- "If you seek him, he will be found by you, but if you forsake him, he will forsake you." 2 Chronicles 15:2b
- "Seek the Lord while he may be found, call upon Him while he is near; let the wicked forsake his way, and the unrighteous man his thoughts; let him return to the Lord, that he may have mercy on him, and to our God, for he will abundantly pardon. Isaiah 55:6-7
- "You will seek me and find me; when you seek me with all your heart," Jeremiah 29:13
- "Seek the Lord, all you humble of the land, who do his commands; seek righteousness, seek humility; perhaps you may be hidden on the day of the wrath of the Lord." Zephaniah 2:3
- ". . . seek, and you will find; knock, and it will be opened to you." Jesus said that, Luke 11:9b
- ** "He made from one every nation of men to live on all the face of the earth, having determined allotted periods and the boundaries of their habitation, that they should seek God, in the hope that they might feel after him and find him. Yet he is not far from each one of us," Acts 17:26-27 (The MAIN PURPOSE of life.)

Choose Jesus and His Word, they are Alive. See also "What's in it For Me" note 28.

153

CHARACTER TYPES

Just as there are many animals in the jungle, so there are many "Character Types" in humanity. Some C.T.'s are good, some not so good. And this list is by no means complete. . .:

- Thief – "What is yours is mine . . ."
- Con/Scam artist – "The more lies the merrier".
- Workaholic – These folks have to be moving and producing all the time.
- Athlete – Much physical activity & energy for sports & competition.
- The animal lover/rescuer – A college grad piano teacher of mine had 40 animals in her apartment (w/o landlord's knowledge or consent.)
- Alcoholic/drug addict – It is said that every family has a person who falls victim to alc. or drugs – and many of them just die.
- Gambler/spender – these folks cannot control their money, so it controls them.
- Miser/hoarder – holding on to all things "tightly".
- The activist – These folks go after some society problem to the point of obsession to the cause.
- The worrywart – always fearful about something to the point of paranoia. Not satisfied unless they find a problem issue to worry about.
- The atheist – Focuses on numerous reasons/arguments why they think faith in the Biblical God is false. They can be intellectual & convincing like C. Darwin & S. Hawking.

In Scripture there are some of the above types, but "boiling down" all of humanity, we see only two: The <u>first</u> Adam or "Jack of the dust"; the <u>last</u> Adam or Jesus Christ which is the character type from heaven. "Thus, it is written, the first man Adam became a living being; the last Adam became a life-giving spirit ... The first man was from the earth, a man of dust; the second man is from heaven." 1 Corinthians 15:45,47 According to Bible scholars, the 1st Adam is <u>the fountain of sin and death</u>, he began the natural character type which is isolated from God's blessing (Ephesians 4:17-18). The second Adam is the <u>fountain of righteousness and life.</u> Those who follow the "second Adam" are blessed & move upward toward a better destiny. "whoever drinks of the water that I shall give him will never thirst: the water that I shall give him will become in him a spring of water welling up to eternal life." Jesus Christ, John 4:14

Now we live in a world of many religions and religious leaders. Jesus the Christ is the only one that rose from the dead to prove all His teachings & claims. (This G-note is written on Easter Sunday, March '17) And the New Testament is generous enough to EXPLAIN how Jesus is the second or last Adam character type. It also explains in great detail the work & functions of Jesus as our advocate, mediator, & priest. Then it explains how we all need to connect with Him before we go out into eternity "naked", without the "robe" of God's only authorized salvation. (See "Rude Surprises" note 79). "How shall we escape if we neglect such a great salvation? It was declared at first by the Lord, and it was attested to us by those who heard him". Hebrews 2:3

There is an old nursery rhyme that I find interesting:

Jack and Jill went up the hill, To fetch a pail of water.
Jack fell down and broke his crown, And Jill came tumbling after.

This may speak of the original man (Adam) pursuing good things, but stumbles with temptation taking all others down with him. Scripture says we are all fallen creatures –"all have sinned & come short of the glory of God," Romans 3:23 The second Adam makes it easy for us all, "I am the light of the world; he who follows me will not walk in darkness, but will have the light of life." Jesus Christ, John 8:12

To finish I simply ask, are you a Jack or Jill of the lower "dust", or are you a Jack of the higher "dust"? "Just as we have borne the image of the man of dust, we shall also (let us) bear the image of the man of heaven". 1 Corinthians 15:49 Choose Jesus, He is Alive. See also "Gifts & Rifts", note 90 for another look at human character.

154

SERENITY

Serenity is an ideal that is rare in this hard & stressful world. The best definition is right from Webster as "not disturbed or troubled, calm, peaceful, tranquil, quiet etc." Easily one could say that Serenity is one of those "Elusive Things" (note 8) this world is good at neutralizing. But nearly all have heard of the "Serenity Prayer":

God grant me the serenity to accept the things I cannot change,
courage to change the things I can; and wisdom to know the difference.
Living one day at a time; enjoying one moment at a time; accepting
hardships as the pathway to peace.
Taking, as Jesus did, this sinful world as it is, not as I would have it.
Trusting that He will make all things right if I surrender to His Will.
That I may be reasonably happy in this life and supremely happy with
Him forever in the next. Amen.
-Reinhold Niebuhr

Now this was written by a liberal Protestant theologian several decades ago. It contains good points, and misleading ones. That part about "accepting things" and "courage to change" is off base BECAUSE the beauty of true Christianity is that God's Spirit in our lives gives us the power to change for the better – not just courage to do it ourselves. That approach is condemned in Scripture as salvation by works – Ephesians 2:8-9 (below). Living & Enjoying one day & moment at a time is commendable – too many folks live in the past or in the future. We should live in the present, thinking Godly thoughts Philippians 4:8, and of course pray for our needs – it's a priceless benefit of Christ's salvation package. Philippians 4:6.

"Accepting hardships as the pathway to peace", speaks of a mysterious Divine principle we see in 2 Corinthians 12:10 "For the sake of Christ, then, I am content with weaknesses, insults, hardships, persecutions, and calamities; for when I am weak, then I am strong." Many folks never understand this, but some do – see Psalms 25:14

Now when R. Niebuhr says that "Jesus took this sinful world as it is", he was speaking with a lame liberal forked tongue. Jesus Christ always made an uncompromising stand for truth. He also claimed to be the SOURCE of change & Hope & serenity. John 14:6

I appreciate Niebuhr's conclusion "Trusting that He will make all things right if I surrender to His Will." A more recent theologian said, "The surrender of the will is the <u>key</u> to becoming a Christian, and the secret to living a victorious Christian life."[9] Dr. Bill Bright That sounds like moving SELF from the throne of one's life & asking Jesus to be on the throne. It's only then we can have those BENEFITS – "That I may be reasonably happy in this life and supremely happy with Him forever in the next." That's serenity.

- Ephesians 2:8-9 – "For by grace you have been saved through faith; and this is not your own doing, it is the gift of God – not because of works, lest any man should boast."
- Philippians 4:8 – "Finally, brethren, whatever is true, whatever is honorable, whatever is just, whatever is pure, whatever is lovely, whatever is gracious, if there is any excellence, if there is anything worthy of praise, think about these things."
- Philippians 4:6 – "Have no anxiety about anything, but in everything by prayer and supplication with thanksgiving let your requests be made known to God."
- Psalms 25:14 KJV – "The secret of the Lord is with them that fear him, and he will shew them his covenant."
- John 14:6 – "Jesus said to him, 'I am the way, and the truth, and the life; no one comes to the Father, but by me."

Choose Jesus, He is Alive, and His own gift of serenity can be yours: John 14:27 – "Peace I leave with you; my peace I give to you; not as the world gives do I give to you. Let not your hearts be troubled, neither let them be afraid."

155

I DON'T EAT PORK

Typically, when we hear the above statement it means someone has made a religious connection. Especially a Jewish or Islamic connection. But when it's mentioned in a Christian context it's usually a bit off base. Now it is human nature to rally around something when we want to sooth the conscience & feel righteous. Some other religious rallying positions besides not eating pork are these:

- no dancing or partying
- no jewelry or fancy hair styles-many sects promote this
- no money – vows of poverty
- no marriage – celibate priests, monks, nuns, etc.
- community service is a common conscience soother
- animal rescue is almost a religion for some
- special Holy days must be recognized
- special underwear must be worn – LDS
- special hats or beards or shaved heads
- burkas or red spot between eyes must be worn

The above positions, and title above can be salvation by works. That is where individuals (& or) organized groups feel a need to earn right standing with God (righteousness or clean conscience). This human thinking is "old as dirt", but is it God's revealed plan for this age??

The world has an ancient Book that divides time & history into two parts: Old Testament and New Testament. Some pages of the O.T. can lead to strict diet restrictions, polygyny, even ethnic cleansing, and other odd customs. (Such Moses era cases of "service to God" can be found in Deuteronomy, 2 Samuel & Joshua.) The O.T. is wonderful but needs to be carefully interpreted. The main point of the New Testament is that Jesus Christ has simplified the whole process of salvation. It is now a GIFT from above provided by the sacrifice of Christ, which we can willingly receive or shun. Our common works or efforts to please God as per the above (very incomplete) list may be fine, good, & wholesome but count for little or nothing as payment for our salvation.

Shortly after the resurrection of Christ the apostles still had Old Testament Jewish restrictions of diet & ceremonial issues in mind but Peter had a mysterious & dynamic vision of all animals & birds that were now

O.K. to eat (Acts 10:9-16). That incident changed the O.T. rules on meat eating taboos, and other ancient policies. For those who can accept the New Testament as Scripture, we now live in an era of freedom from dead works, and enjoy salvation by grace, (& pork – any way you like it).

- Ephesians 2:8-9 "For by grace you have been saved through faith; and this is not your own doing, it is the gift of God – not because of works, lest any man should boast."
- Romans 7:6 "But now we are discharged from the Law, dead to that which held us captive, so that we serve not under the old written code but in the new life of the Spirit."
- Romans 14:2 & 5 "One believes he may eat anything, while the weak man eats only vegetables. . . One man esteems one day as better than another, while another man esteems all days alike. Let everyone be fully convinced in his own mind."
- Galatians 5:1 "For freedom Christ has set us free; stand fast therefore, and do not submit again to a yoke of slavery."
- 1 Corinthians 15:3 "For I delivered to you as of first importance what I also received, that Christ died for our sins in accordance with the Scriptures."
- 1 Peter 1:23 "You have been born anew, not of perishable seed but of imperishable, through the living and abiding Word of God;"

As a test just try reading/living the Word of God & see if satanic opposition doesn't come out of nowhere to take the Word habit from you. . . Same with New Testament church attendance. Same with the prayer habit. But there will be no satanic opposition for social & religious games as per incomplete list above. Our adversary has always approved of misguided zeal & religious confusion.

Choose Jesus & His practical salvation. Other approaches to God can be too complicated and lead to dead end paths, & "Rude Surprises" note 79. See also note 9, "Serving God".

156

DIVINE PRIORITIES

We all have our priorities, so would God have priorities? Is there a Divine system or schedule that is all around us, in every age? About 4,000 years ago Abraham & Israel were dramatically started. God made promises to them (and not to other ancient nations), that He would bless & make Israel great (Genesis 12:1-2). About 2,000 years ago the followers of Christ were likened to Israel (Romans 2:29 & Galatians 6:15-16), which makes the Christian a micro type of the macro nation of Israel w/its priority position w/God.

A few Divine Priorities questions WHY: (and yes, I do have more questions than answers.)

- Why did God treat Israel differently?
- Why do many young Christians get extra care & special treatment which older ones often seem to lack? (Hebrews 1:14)
- Why are some folk's prayers answered quicker?
- Why are miracles shown to some & not others? (Matthew 9:29 – Jesus)
- Why do some live in chaos & despair, from crisis to crisis?
- Why are some folks blessed & others don't appear to be?

Cover to cover the Bible reveals the nature of a God which draws near to those who actively seek Him. It's also God's nature to move away from sinners & those who reject or have no time for Him - "Divine Priorities" . . . It appears to be politically correct to believe in a big sweet universal grandfather type God, but the Bible knows nothing of that distortion. Among other things, "Divine Priorities" may explain why praying for oneself can often be answered quickly, while praying for others may take longer to see God's answer – maybe MUCH longer. (And in our atheistic day & age the liberals have smeared the glory of Christ, and undermined the integrity of the Scriptures, so we are set up for spiritual confusion & apathy, & ignorance of Divine Priorities.)

For "no extra charge" here is a "cruise ship" illustration: Someone willing & able to put me on an expensive but FREE ocean voyage with all the amenities such as premium food, nice private cabin, entertainment, pools & hot tubs, interesting ports, etc. Would that benefactor force me to go if I was sitting stubborn, cross armed with back towards the ship saying, "H__ no, I won't go." Many folks treat God exactly the same way, when they hear the Gospel & benefits of Christ's salvation. (See "What's in It For Me?" note 28)

- Psalms 18:25-26 "With the loyal thou dost show thyself loyal; with the blameless man thou dost show thyself blameless; With the pure thou dost show thyself pure; and with the crooked thou dost show thyself perverse."
- Isaiah 55:8-9 KJV "My thoughts are not your thoughts, neither are your ways my ways, saith the Lord. For as the heavens are higher than the earth, so are my ways higher than your ways, and my thoughts than your thoughts."
- Matthew 11:25-26 "Jesus declared . . . Father . . . thou has hidden these things from the wise and understanding and revealed them to babes . . ." (a matter of election & depth of experience.)
- Luke 8:18 "Take heed then how you hear; for to him who has will more be given, and from him who has not, even what he thinks that he has will be taken away." (Jesus Christ said that.)
- 1 Corinthians 1:27-29 "God chose what is foolish in the world to shame the wise, God chose what is weak in the world to shame the strong, God chose what is low and despised in the world, even things that are not, to bring to nothing things that are, so that no human being might boast in the presence of God."

Well if there are Divine Priorities, and a God who chooses & blesses some & not others, I want to get in on the good side of that action. How about you? Choose Jesus, He is Alive & ABLE to save from godless living, the second death, & hell. See also "The Blessing & The Curse" note 66.

157

<u>HAPPY FACTS OF LIFE</u>

Several years ago, I wrote the "Sad Facts" title (note 19) which needs to be balanced to lessen the sour grapes in this "Gospel Note" series. And when I think of all the goodies God has put into life, and the way the Divine connection improves & completes the human, there is plenty to be happy about:

- God truly exists and wishes to hear us when we pray to Him.
- The Bible is true & contains thousands of promises for our best interest.
- God does not play favorites. He is impartial to all that come to Him on His terms.
- Miracles still happen. I have experienced several. See "My Miracles" note 33.
- God hears you when you cry. Angels are present when you die.
- It is possible to have good success if you apply the formula: Self-Discipline + Knowledge + Work + Money Management + FAITH = Success/Freedom. See "Formula for Success" note 83.
- Dreams can come true along with some "story book" fantasies.
- Storms pass over after a while.
- Santa Claus exists in the form of our Lord Jesus. See "Santa Claus" note 127.
- God invented dogs for people who are burned out on people. Mark Twain said, "The more I learn about people, the more I like my dog." (I'm not sure why God invented cats.)
- The active presence of God enhances life in many ways such as emotional victory, miracles, divine guidance, physical healing & strength, joyfulness, answered prayer, confidence & others. Christians can cultivate that Divine presence by prayer, Bible study & worship/ fellowship, and rejection of sin & hypocrisy. See "Divine Presence" note 73.
- The Gospel (first ref. below) is the central theme of the New Testament, and it's clear as day for those who are willing to accept it.

The truth of the above "list" is often blocked from many who <u>need to know</u> those things. The "world" offers a package of salvation/hope that is false & hollow and fails people at the time they need it most – life's sad end. Things such as money, vibrant youth, health & beauty, warm social engagement, self-actualization, pride, etc. can be misleading & lack long term "happiness". And we live in a modern world that tries it's best to drown out the simple & clear Gospel message that Christ's salvation brings light & God's blessing & eternal life in heaven. The following "thoughts" from New & Old Testament Scripture give a picture of God's better plan for us:

- 1 Corinthians 15:3-5 "For I delivered to you as of first importance what I also received, that Christ died for our sins in accordance with the Scriptures, that he was buried, that he was raised on the third day in accordance with the Scriptures, and that he appeared to Cephas, then to the twelve."
- Proverbs 18:24 "There are friends who pretend to be friends, but there is a friend who sticks closer than a brother." (That would be Jesus Christ & His Spirit.)
- Psalms 84:11 "For the Lord God is a sun and shield; he bestows favor and honor. No good thing does the Lord withhold from those who walk uprightly."
- Lamentations 3:25 "The Lord is good to those who wait for him, to the soul that seeks him."
- Romans 8:18 "I consider that the sufferings of this present time are not worth comparing with the glory that is to be revealed to us."
- Romans 8:31 KJV ". . . If God be for us, who can be against us?"

With the Bible as it is FULL of revealed truth and "Happy Facts of Life", we can all be encouraged. But sincerely accepting Christ's salvation is the way to make it real. "Behold, I stand at the door and knock; if anyone hears my voice and opens the door, I will come in to him and eat with him, and he with me." Revelation 3:20 Choose Jesus, He is Alive.

158

WHY I WRITE

I was in Viet Nam in the early 70's & became so pathologically depressed I was VERY suicidal. (More V.N. vets have passed to suicide than were killed in the conflict.) At the "darkest" point I resolved to give the "Jesus saves" thing a try before pulling the trigger. If it was real, I would live it – and it was more than I expected. From the beginning of my "drawing nigh to God" (James 4:8) experiment, there has been lots of mysterious & penetrating spiritual "stuff" in my life. The Holy Spirit manifested Himself at the start & miracles happened. I had a kind of "high" for weeks, & it would be rejuvenated in Wed. nite fellowship meetings. I was still in the active U.S. Army at the time but got out w/honorable discharge. A few years passed & I re-entered the Army as a Chaplain Assistant.

Being offered a Key West assignment was hard not to like. Only the chaplains there were liberal as they get. A Methodist, a Lutheran, & a young Catholic priest, & they all gave me the cold shoulder because I was a Bible believer. My Methodist boss chaplain was NOT fond of the Scriptures or committed to Biblical thought. Well, there is a "balance in nature" & my Gospel-notes started there. Some of the soldiers & sailors said my "notes" were "anointed". My liberal chaplains may not have felt that way & I was more or less "fired". And God gave me a better assignment. (See "The Chaplains" note 70.)

Over the years my writing "Gospel Notes" mostly happens when I feel moved by the Spirit & not all are "happy morsels of truth" – some may be "inflammatory" – (a Calvinist w/a doctorate told me that, but he also called me "Freddy the flea" & "stupid thing", so I can't take his "word" seriously). But I do try to write positive essays more than negative ones. I write BECAUSE:

1. My Born Again experience & renewal in Christ may be of rare quality judging by the spiritual "stuff" God has revealed to ME, (& I don't claim to have charming social vibrations - I do not write to get inroads in the church.) I just want to share this Gospel material & help others to "connect". And when some accuse me of lying, it's O.K. – Jesus Christ himself was horribly rejected & murdered by a conspiracy. At least I know how He felt – John 1:11.
2. On the night of my "Come to Jesus" experience, there was a blood vision revealed to me ("What's in the Blood" note 96). Then five years

later ("I Saw the King" note 7). Those two events are something like a commission to me.

3. I like putting a wholesome element into the internet since so much of cyberspace appears to be demon possessed. But closer to home, this series will be bound in book form for my kids & grandkids to know me better.
4. And then generally, I enjoy writing gospel tracts & it may be my gift.

- 2 Corinthians 5:17 "If anyone is in Christ, he is a new creation: the old has passed away, behold, the new has come."
- Romans 1:16 "I am not ashamed of the gospel: it is the power of God for salvation to everyone who has faith, to the Jew first and also to the Greek."
- John 14:6 "Jesus said, "I am the way, and the truth, and the life; no one comes to the Father, but by me."

Well, that's "Why I Write" Gospel-notes. Considering the change Jesus made in my life (I would now be dead otherwise), I KNOW that ALL need to take the Bible & its salvation message seriously. Choose Jesus, He is Alive. See also "Faith" note 75 & 43 "The Demon".

159

INVISIBLE SUPPORT

Support is a basic fact of life in this world. A chair has to have legs. A car has to have wheels. A tree has to have a trunk. The house roof has to have walls to hold it up. Etc. etc. Then looking at human psychological & practical needs, there must be support systems. Without support systems people are or feel lost & insecure. The standard support system is one's family & circle of friends which give good "social vibrations", which is necessary & maybe vital. Other support systems are:

- School associates whether Grade School, H.S., or College
- Church groups & affiliation
- The hippy culture of the 60's & 70's was a classic S.S. (did it go away?)
- LGBT culture is a support system (but in Orlando they have serious problems)
- Motorcycle clubs are a typical S.S.
- National folks such as Jewish, Asian, Jamaican, Chinatowns, some immigrants - these typical groups can hang together as support systems (but not Americans as we tend to be "Cannibals" note 29)
- Animal lovers have a S.S. with their pets because there is unconditional love/support there
- Internet & Facebook connection for young & old – another classic S.S.

But what about "Invisible Support"?? The New Testament & Jesus Christ reveal the most classic Biblical Support System, and it amounts to "Invisible Support". It is MORE than a religious belief system – it's based on a RELATIONSHIP with Jesus Christ (who is also invisible). And it really is like pulling things out of the air. Of course, the world sees a farce or "immaculate deception", but the relationship with Jesus can be felt – if not immediate, then in a short while after one makes a sincere adult decision for Christ & His atonement.

Now the church is where Christian believers belong, and they should get the relationship teaching there. They should also get a wholesome social support system. But I believe "Invisible Support" goes above & beyond church involvement/attendance. It doesn't replace church, it's what the Born-Again believer should take with him that 99% of time he is not inside the walls of the church. "Invisible Support" & relationship w/J.C. encompasses the core issues of salvation: deliverance, safety, preservation, healing, & soundness (Scofield). But also, brotherhood, confidence in God, emotional victory, answered prayer, feeling Divine presence & guidance, prosperity, and comfort from above. Yes, that's all a tall order but it can be and IS what the Book teaches. And the Christian can have it with him/her 24-7. That's "Invisible Support", and that's why I write "Gospel Notes". God's salvation is good stuff, NOT junk. My experience of 45 years. Thank you, Jesus.

- 2 Chronicles 16:9a KJV "the eyes of the Lord run to and fro throughout the whole earth, to shew himself strong in the behalf of them whose heart is perfect toward him."
- Psalms 25:14 "The friendship of the Lord is for those who fear him, and he makes known to them his covenant."
- Psalms 94:19 "When the cares of my heart are many, thy consolations cheer my soul."
- Habakkuk 3:19 KJV "The Lord God is my strength, and he will make my feet like hinds' feet, and he will make me to walk upon mine high places."
- 1 Corinthians 1:18 "For the word of the cross is folly to those who are perishing, but to us who are being saved it is the power of God."
- 2 Timothy 1:7 KJV "For God hath not given us the spirit of fear; but of power, and of love, and of a sound mind."
- 1 Peter 3:12 "The eyes of the Lord are upon the righteous, and his ears are open to their prayer. But the face of the Lord is against those that do evil."

I realize this Gospel Note doesn't mention eternal life & hell, just the "living it" part of Christianity (which is the hard part). But if we get the temporal right, the "final transition" will certainly take care of itself, and eternal life in Heaven is said to be premium, fine, & good. Choose Jesus, He is Alive. "Behold, I stand at the door and knock; if anyone hears my voice and opens the door, I will come in to him and eat with him, and he with me." Rev. 3:20 See note 28 "What's in It For Me".

160

THE NATURE OF OUR ADVERSARY

By "adversary" I am referring to the Biblical character "the serpent", "the devil", or "Lucifer". The world presents a silly & false image of anything Biblical which makes believing difficult. And I too would rather not believe in such a character, but satanic activity is becoming too obvious. It possesses people, then promotes bizarre traits & actions. Our natural human desires can be magnified & altered into evil contortions. And it's amazing to see people globally following a false concept of God into total self-destruction & mass murder. The "Nature of Our Adversary" has to be powerful & beautiful to lure people the way it does. Then in the end (likely near), the majority will be so charmed that they worship the adversary – Revelation 13.

Scripture reveals "the serpent" in Genesis 4 as Eve's tempter. People often ridicule "the talking snake" of Genesis. But there are other instances of addressing Satan through another entity, like when Jesus Christ told Peter to "get behind me Satan", in Matthew chapter 16 v.23a. That exchange gives a penetrating look at the "Nature of Our Adversary". 23b gives this: "You are an offense to Me, for you are not mindful of the things of God, but the things of men". Right there we have the practical nature of our spiritual adversary. This supernatural character persuades humans to highlight self-focus. We excessively dwell on our Pride, Possessions, Power, and Honor (note 41), rather than looking for ANSWERS above & seeking God, the true purpose of life. (Other direct & revealing references to the Nature of Our Adversary are Job 1:6-7, Zechariah 3:1-2, and Matthew 4:1-11.)

Besides having a very human agenda, & contradicting God/good constantly, what is he like?? Well, not only is he a supernatural entity in a higher dimension, but he almost resembles God by being a three-part being: The father - (Lucifer, Isaiah 14:12-15 KJV, Ezekiel 28:12-15.) The son? - (demons, fallen angels who still possess people today, and certainly that end time character of Revelation 13.) The spirit - "the prince of the power of the air, the spirit who now works in the sons of disobedience." Ephesians 2:2 (Of course we cannot fully understand ANY spiritual being, but a study of Scripture does reveal a hierarchy of evil, or chain of command, & network of dark spiritual powers.) And its sad when unchurched young people don't understand or believe the subtle reality & power our adversary has. They fall for "supernatural" themes of the youth culture, and find themselves living the desires of the devil which are: "immorality, impurity, licentiousness, idolatry, sorcery, enmity, strife, jealousy, anger, selfishness, dissention, party spirit, envy, murder, drunkenness, carousing, and the like." Galatians 5:19-21

In spite of the OBVIOUS increasing evil & demonic activity in our troubled world, too many folks stubbornly reject Biblical answers & give complacent consent to living under the power of our adversary. Scripture defined the predicament some 2000 years ago: Paul's mission from the ascended & glorified Jesus – "to open their eyes, that they may turn from darkness to light and from the power of Satan to God, that they may receive forgiveness of sins and a place among those who are sanctified by faith in me." Acts 26:18 When I was about 21, I had my epiphany & made a decision for Christ & broke free of the desires of the worldly spirit as per above. Feeling the Holy Spirit & NEW direction in my life caused curiosity to study & figure out things most folks don't bother with. The result is this "gospel note" on "The Nature of Our Adversary", and indeed the whole GOSPEL NOTES series. And I am not ashamed to make literalistic conclusions on this subject. The alternative liberal conclusions on the Word of God have surely paved the way for spiritual blindness & the free reign of evil in the world today.

Now according to Scripture, and the Biblical world view, we are the puppets of a raging good vs. evil battle where our souls are at stake. For spiritual survival tips see Ephesians 6 which deals with the Armor of God. And choose Jesus, He is Alive. See also note 43 "The Demon" and note 110 "What's in the Air".

161

LIBERAL THEOLOGY

This essay is not in support but against Liberal Theology. I believe our modern world has an anti-Bible & anti-Christ spirit which engineers & promotes L.T. If the purpose of life is to find truth & God (Acts 17:26-27) and be Biblically saved, then these are perilous times because of L.T. in the religious arena. Now it's natural for folks to stand between liberal & conservative positions & choose w/o knowing many of the arguments either way. We choose sometimes at random, but usually from family traditions or friendships. Which means people may not know what they're getting into.

It is commonly believed that L.T. takes away faith. (This makes sense since many liberals are ashamed to believe – see "God's Not Dead" note 142.) Especially in the seminary where the graduate school profs. have masters & doctorate degrees – how could they be wrong on Bible doctrine? And why wouldn't our adversary "the serpent" infiltrate seminaries w/ educated but deniers of time-honored doctrines & creeds? (Although, the Church was warned of this problem even before the Apostles passed. See 2 Peter 2:1)

The early years of the last century was the main era of doctrinal challenge. Conservative beliefs & creeds were bashed by mostly German theologians & philosophers such as: Paul Tillich, S.A. Kierkegaard, Adolf Harnack, H.E. Fosdick, David F. Strauss, Henry Ware, & Albrecht Ritschl. They came to this country & resumed their teaching careers at our leading colleges & seminaries. Their "new" & liberal theology challenged things like the Nature of God & the Trinity, the Deity & Lordship of Jesus Christ AND HIS ATONEMENT, the authority & sanctity of Scripture, miracles & even the RESURRECTION of Christ. There was some resistance in the Church, but faithless, & Christ denying doctrines took hold in the name of "modernism". To this day about half of the Catholic & Protestant leaders are liberal. And I have known a few. They offer no legitimate Gospel of a heaven to gain or hell to shun by the merits of Jesus Christ.

I think on the subject of theology and our eternal souls, it is better to be safe than sorry. I know it can be tough to make a stand for Christ & those strange words "saved" & "salvation". Conservative Bible "thumpers" have been criticized by man for thousands of years. BUT - God has given us his view of loose/liberal handling of revealed Divine truth:

- 1 Samuel 15:23 KJV "For rebellion is as the sin of witchcraft, and stubbornness is as iniquity and idolatry. Because thou has rejected the word of the Lord, he hath also rejected thee from being king". Samuel's word from God to Saul 1050 BC.
- Proverbs 19:27 KJV "Cease, my son, to hear the instruction that causeth to err from the words of knowledge." 950 B.C.
- Jeremiah 7:24 "But they did not obey or incline their ear, but walked in their own counsels and the stubbornness of their evil hearts, and went backward and not forward." 626 B.C.
- Matthew 10:33 "But whoever denies me before men, I also will deny before my Father who is in heaven." Jesus said that.
- Colossians 2:8 KJV "Beware lest any man spoil you through philosophy and vain deceit, after the tradition of men, after the rudiments of the world, and not after Christ."
- 2 John 9 "Anyone who goes ahead and does not abide in the doctrine of Christ does not have God; he who abides in the doctrine of Christ has both the Father and the Son."

D.C. Hodge: "No road to perdition has ever been more thronged than that of false doctrine. Error is a shield over the conscience and a bandage over the eyes."[6] The tragedy & deadly part of Liberal Theology is after it is drilled into people's heads, and with the majority of the world as a chorus of "One World & Religious Tolerance", liberals hang with their un-Biblical/Christ rejecting religion till time pulls them under - without Christ's salvation. And there are no air conditioners in hell.

- *LIBERAL THEOLOGY & ETERNITY: If wrong, devotees lose their souls. If right, devotees gain nothing.*
    - ❖ *NO WAY TO WIN*
- *CONSERVATIVE THEOLOGY & ETERNITY: If wrong, devotees lose nothing. If right, devotees gain heaven.*
    - ❖ *NO WAY TO LOSE*

Besides gaining heaven, conservative Christians also get blessed by God while they live. It's a better deal. Choose Jesus, He is Alive. See also "Waxing Liberal" note 112.

162

THE FACE PLANT

What is a Face Plant? Is it a plant or a flower that looks like a human or animal face? No – it's a high stakes "college try" or "do or die trying" endeavor where failure happens along with injuries & losses. It's where we attempt to do something extra cool to possibly make up for past mistakes, only to add one more big failure to the collection. The Face Plant is a matter of driving too hard to achieve career, romance, estate, business growth, etc. and then have a bold failure. And I'm sure ALL of us have a fiasco situation burned in our memory from a distant experience or a recent one.

I believe our WANTS & DESIRES can lead to obsession but our desires can be misleading, & even sincere religious folks can read into a situation, by way of hunches & feelings & signs, etc., of God's endorsement/blessing when it's not really there. God generally helps people with NEEDS – not wants. We should know the difference. If there is too much uncertainty, it may be an indication that God isn't for our plan. It may be just an Obsession (note 61), or Illusion (note 80). I find that usually a steady peace in a situation is a better sign of Divine agreement.

Now in the Bible we have examples of the Face Plant. Below are three that led to death, and three that led to therapy & cleansing for the characters involved:

- Balaam – A heathen diviner that was hired by a local king to curse the early Israelites. It led to his demise. Numbers 22-24
- Belshaz'zar – A king who had an extreme pride/ego & died "driving hard." Daniel 5
- Judas – Just false & greedy but had one of the world's worst fatal Face Plants. Acts 1:18
- King David – His devious seduction of an officer's wife & termination of Uri'ah the officer was David's Face Plant, but it humbled him & shaped his devotional character. 2 Samuel 11 He rebounded to write most of the Psalms.
- Peter – Was maybe the boldest disciple of Jesus Christ, but Face Planted when he denied Christ at His trial. Matthew 26:34-35 Rebounded to lead the early church.
- Paul – Had Christians arrested & some murdered but Face Planted on

the road to Damascus. Acts 9 He rebounded to be the intellectual mind of the New Covenant.

Now I've been told by police officers that police dogs are trained to WIN every time, which gives them a cocky attitude. Well, some Christian & religious folks may need a Face Plant now & then for "therapy & cleansing" of their "hard driving" attitude. BUT the humbling Face Plant can have long lasting repercussions & regrets, so how do we get closure? How to count losses & move on? I think this is where FAITH, PRAYER, and SCRIPTURE can be <u>greatly</u> helpful. We should ask God for <u>peace & healing</u> in the memory of the situation <u>whenever</u> it raises its ugly head. Example: "Lord, this thing has eaten me up for a long time, please heal by Your power & I will be grateful and help me to NOT repeat the mistake."

- "When pride cometh, then cometh shame; but with the lowly is wisdom." Proverbs 11:2 KJV
- "Keep your life free from love of money and be content with what you have; for he has said, 'I will never fail you nor forsake you." Hebrews 13:5
- "Come now, you who say, 'Tomorrow we will go into such and such a town and spend a year there and trade and get gain', whereas you do not know about tomorrow. What is your life? For you are a mist that appears for a little time and then vanishes." James 4:13-14
- "If we confess our sins, he is faithful and just, and will forgive our sins and cleans us from all unrighteousness. 1 John 1:9

This Gospel Note is my "eating crow" message (which cost me a "munch of bunny" to learn the lesson). But it still needs an "appeal" to the reader. Are <u>you</u> moving toward God & able to see <u>the wisdom</u> of humility, & hazards of excess ambition?? Then Choose Jesus, He is Alive. And the Christian value system will become like "treasure hidden in a field" Matthew 13:44, which <u>you</u> found.

163

TO BE OR NOT TO BE

Prince Hamlet of Shakespeare said, "To be, or not to be, this is the question." Well, on a higher-level people should say, "To Believe, or Not to Believe, this is the question." So, what does it mean "to believe"? According to Webster it means to like or desire. Also, to take as true or real, and to have confidence in a statement or promise of another person. The Bible is thought to be the "statement or promises" of a "person" called God.

The things of God such as purpose, benefits, destiny, etc. are revealed in the "statement or promises" of God, (the Word). So naturally we come to the Word or record of thousands of years of fascinating events & materials on God's dealings with those who "believed", (and those who did not believe). Of course when we decide to like or desire God and look into the Book we find "repent and believe" Mark 1:15, which is a matter of changing one's life purpose of pride & ego & self focus, to a relationship with Jesus Christ & God's revealed program – John 3:16. Many years ago I personally approached Biblical truth "to believe", & God confirmed my faith with Divine Presence (note 73), & several miracles (note 33). But some expect God to change, which may be why there is so much darkness & religious confusion in the world.

Then "to believe" what? Our intellectual pride says, "I can't buy that story . . ." Well, could it be that God tests us by putting hard to believe miracles in the Book to see who will believe Him & who will not believe Him?? Could a lot of miracles be an affiliation test?? And when we start tossing miracles & material from the Book, it's anybody's guess where that will end – liberals even reject the Biblical core teachings (derived from miracles) such as virgin birth, sacrificial death, resurrection, & ascension of Jesus Christ. And Jesus is the most amazing miracle of the Bible, but when the miraculous is rejected His Deity & Lordship typically goes too. I've heard some liberal clergy say with disbelief & disgust, "Ha, Jesus was just a man." I personally don't care who thinks I'm simple minded, those miracles are a beautiful & essential part of the Book – all of them.

Below are a few Scripture refs. which touch the matter of "believing". Let the Word of God speak for itself. . .

- Genesis 15:6 "And he (Abraham) believed the Lord; and He reckoned it to him as righteousness." (This is the ROOT of saving faith which

Paul the apostle completely explains in the book of Romans.)

- John 3:16 "For God so loved the world that he gave his only Son, that whoever believes in him should not perish but have eternal life."
- Romans 4:13-14 "The promise to Abraham . . . did not come through the law (of Moses) but through the righteousness of faith (believing).
- Romans 10:9 "because, if you confess with your lips that Jesus is Lord and believe in your heart that God raised him from the dead, you will be saved." (There's that affiliation & miraculous element . . .)
- Romans 15:13 "May the God of hope fill you with all joy and peace in believing, so that by the power of the Holy Spirit you may abound in hope."
- Hebrews 11:6 "And without faith it is impossible to please him. For whoever would draw near to God must believe that he exists and that he rewards those who seek him."
- Jude 5b ". . . that he who saved a people out of the land of Egypt, afterward destroyed those who did not believe."

The sum total of those references is a matter of being "in Christ", which is what believing Biblical truth does for us. And those rewards mentioned just above amount to God's purpose, benefits, & destiny. Things like living to please one's creator, reaping Biblical benefits while alive on this planet (note 28), and being an heir of heaven (instead of hell) forever. Good stuff – priceless in fact . . . Choose Jesus, He is Alive. See also "Faith", note 75.

164

<u>EXODUS 20</u>

This short chapter of the Bible is probably the most amazing of all Bible chapters. It contains miraculous drama of the highest quality ever. God speaking from a mountain top to over a million trembling Israelites with Moses mediating between God and the people. It is exactly where we find the 10 commandments of God. Exodus 20 is not the first dramatic revealing of the power & majesty of God. The book of Genesis has plenty of the earliest miracles, but the Exodus has to be among the best revelations of God's glory & power. He identified Himself in a way that would get the early Israelite's attention – 10 plagues on Egypt, parting of Red Sea, then Mt. Sinai & the 10 commandments from "thundering and the lightning and the sound of the trumpet and the mountain smoking" (Exodus 20:18) & voice of God from the sky.

<u>It's interesting what God had to say</u>: (1) No other gods (2) No idols – God even says He is jealous & will curse & or bless folks for violating or complying. (3) No using God's name in vain. (4) Keep the Sabbath day holy – 6 day creation is confirmed in this commandment (5) Honor father & mother (6) No murder (7) No adultery (8) No stealing (9) No Lying (10) Don't covet neighbors stuff. Exodus 20:1-17 It's also interesting that Scripture explains WHY <u>in the same chapter</u> – "Moses said . . . Do not fear; for God has come to prove you, and that the fear of him may be before your eyes, that you may not sin." Exodus 20:20 (Sin & its consequences are right here in the 10 commandments chapter, especially verse 5 dealing with one's posterity.)

Now today it is commonly believed that God is just loving & kindhearted & not harsh at all, and the strict 10 commandments are just ancient myth. Of course, the New Testament does reveal a Jesus who is LOVE & GRACE incarnate. If Jesus Christ is God in the flesh (and He is), then WHY the CONTRAST?? The Old Testament/Covenant reveals the <u>power</u> & <u>authority</u> & <u>standards</u> & <u>judgment</u> side of God's nature. In Moses' time God was shown more as a strict father who smashed adversaries & troublemakers "like a bug". (see Numbers 16) Strictness & power were necessary to establish the new nation of Israel and stress the importance of accountability to God. The New Testament/Covenant reveals the Son of God who is/becomes the kindhearted "mediator between God & man." (John 3:14; 1 Timothy 2:5-6). This mediator dies for our sins. Jesus shows the love & grace side of God's nature. Neither Old or New Covenants are complete w/o the message of the other. And since the resurrection of Jesus Christ we are all (Jew & Gentile) accountable to the God of the Old & New Testament Scriptures.

Today there are people who say "I go only by the commandments of Moses. Well that's fine & good, but the law of Moses came with hundreds of OTHER rules that made it VERY tough to comply with. And to be Divinely endorsed even then required perfect performance, which was/is impossible. (see "The Endorsement" note 15.)

- Galatians 3:10 "all who rely on works of the law are under a curse; for it is written, "Cursed be everyone who does not abide by all things written in the book of the law, and do them."
- Romans 7:6 "Now we are discharged from the law, dead to that which held us captive, so that we serve not under the old written code but in the new life of the Spirit."

Jesus Christ fulfills the LAW in His person & atonement for sins. Now we can have a personal relationship & know His character of fairness, justice, truth, love, mercy, GRACE, etc. - what the whole Old & New Covenants are getting at. It's not that the old moral code has been canceled. Now it's this: "This is my commandment, that you love one another . . . you are my friends if you do what I command you." John 15:12-14 (For no extra charge, that's the 11th commandment, & the first 10 are still valid).

Well besides the miraculous of Exodus 20 in the Old Testament, we have Jesus Christ in the New Testament. He is the most amazing miracle of the Bible. Being God in the flesh, AND dying for our sin - that's ABOVE & BEYOND any miracle, if you think about it. Choose Jesus, He is Alive.

165

ACRONYMS

This is a word formed from the first letters of a series of words. A classic is RADAR – **R**adio **D**etection **A**nd **R**anging. And there are many acronyms everywhere – esp. in the military. Now there are a few that come to mind. PEJASIS speaks of the sad condition of natural man (and woman).

Pride – the world promotes at least 4 types. See note 45.
Ego – self awareness; conceit; viewing everything in relation to oneself.
Jealousy – being resentfully envious of another's advantages or possessions. This focus leads to devious conduct & hate.
Apostasy – abandoning faith. This appears to be happening too often today. Especially our youth & liberals??
Self **I**nterest – lots of folks live with S.I. as the main purpose of life. They think all should bow to them.
Sin – breaking religious rules or moral principles. Doing what one knows is wrong. However, sin has a way of selling itself – social norms & attitudes, liberal minded habits, etc. Then sin can be all around AND inside our being. I know sin is an embarrassing word, but it still has the hiss of the serpent.

The sum total of PEJASIS is **E**dging **G**od **O**ut (another acronym there). And the above acronym/list surely leaves out a few elements, but humanity is almost defined by those traits. If only those 6 septic traits could be pulled from our race, what would this world be like?? Better for sure, but they won't be pulled soon, so reality says we need an advocate to plead our cause.

Now another acronym is JESUS. This one has the answer to the human condition. (He is the advocate mentioned above.)

-- -- **J**esus **E**xactly **S**uits **U**s **S**inners -- --

Jesus – an iconic character who appeared in history. He lived & died young. BUT is reported to have risen bodily from the dead, which means He is still alive. His name given by an angel BEFORE birth. (For 102 other names of Jesus Christ see "Names of Christ" note 46.)
Exactly – Scripture makes no "bones" about the lost condition of humans & how Christ's atonement is a perfect fit. Acts4:12, Hebrews 2:3 (below)
Suits – to suit means to cover, & that is what the salvation of Jesus Christ

does – a spiritual covering as described in Psalm 91 and by the amazing Apostle Paul. He even uses the analogy of a suit of armor. See Ephesians 6:11-17.

Us – all humanity are in the same sinking boat, infected from birth by the "PEJASIS" problem. Isaiah 53:6 "All we like sheep have gone astray; we have turned away everyone to his own way;" . . .

Sinners – The Old Testament assessment is repeated in the New Testament. Romans 3:23 "All have sinned and come short of the glory of God,"

I think it can be safely said that if one's purpose in life is to be fulfilled & blessed, the two acronyms discussed in this essay are heavy indeed. Humanity is clearly in trouble with our sin natures which block truth, faith, hope, & love of God. The Biblical solution is JESUS who is available to "whosoever will."

- Revelation 3:20 "Behold, I stand at the door and knock; if any one hears my voice and opens the door, I will come in to him and eat with him, and he with me." (Jesus Christ said that.)
- Acts 4:12 "And there is salvation in no one else, for there is no other name (Jesus) under heaven given among men by which we must be saved."
- Hebrews 2:3 "how shall we escape if we neglect such a great salvation? It was declared at first by the Lord, and it was attested to us by those who heard him."
- Hebrews 3:13 "But exhort one another every day, as long as it is called "today," that none of you may be hardened by the deceitfulness of sin."
- Psalm 91:4 "He will cover you with his pinions, (feathers) and under his wings you will find refuge; his faithfulness is a shield and buckler." (God is not a bird – the Bible just uses lots of figures of speech.)
- Jeremiah 29:11 "I know the plans I have for you, says the Lord, plans for welfare and not for evil, to give you a future and a hope."

Choose Jesus, He is Alive. Beat the world system of PEJASIS & be blessed in time & eternity. See also note 114 "Strange Words".

166

EMBRACING

Embracing is a human thing – it means to clasp in the arms lovingly, or to accept readily. Also, to take up or adopt eagerly or seriously. People embrace lovers, hobbies, vocations/professions, philosophies, religions, activist causes, various obsessions, Hollywood, etc. We are known by what we embrace. Someone has said: "What we choose to embrace, what we choose to be responsive to, is the purest reflection of who we are, and what we love." Terryl Givens.

- - Typical Embracings - -

- "Hollywood" is where image & social connections are supreme. (*see Edmund Wilson below)
- Politicians embrace their party platforms & ideals.
- Youth embrace teen idols & culture & often drugs.
- Video gamers embrace a surreal world of drama & action that captivates their minds.
- Tree huggers embrace nature & preservation of the wild.
- Survivalists embrace concepts of self-preservation fearing that this world system will soon crash & burn.
- Most Philosophers & liberals embrace arguments that deny the Biblical God & support unbelief.

While some of the above "embracings" can be legitimate, many of them can be in the "obsessions" category. (see note 61.) And obsessions create an out of balance condition in our lives. Sigmund Freud said this: "A man should not try to eliminate his complexes (an integration of impulses, ideas, & emotions) but to get into accord with them; they are legitimately what directs his conduct in the world."[10] The problem there is continuing the loop of an unhealthy out of balance lifestyle. Embracing some things is a path to frustration & failure. Another problem is embracing the world totally (see "The World" note 27) & pushing away the gospel of Christ.

- LEGITIMATE QUESTIONS

-How many embrace their conscience?

-How many embrace legitimate FAITH?

-How many embrace Jesus & their eternal destiny??

Embracing the conscience & FAITH & Jesus Christ has to be the highest & most legitimate life purpose of all - IF - (1) we all were put in this world to find God & make peace with Him. (2) we all have a SOUL which can be assassinated by unrestrained "embracing" & worldliness – Mark ref. below. (3) we all die at a certain point, and THAT is permanent & final (which appears to be the case). It is said that angels embrace God 24-7 & have the rewards for that devotion. We humans too can enjoy temporal & eternal rewards from devotion & embracing God. That's the whole message of the Bible. It's the gospel in a nutshell.

- Psalm 103:20 KJV "Bless the Lord, ye his angels, that excel in strength, that do his commandments, hearkening unto the voice of his word!"
- Lamentations 3:25-26 "The Lord is good to those who wait for him, to the soul that seeks him. It is good that one should wait quietly for the salvation of the Lord."
- Mark 8:36-37 KJV "For what shall it profit a man, if he shall gain the whole world, and lose his own soul? Or what shall a man give in exchange for his soul?" Jesus Christ said that.
- Ephesians 5:11 "Take no part in the unfruitful works of darkness, but instead expose them."
- 2 Timothy 4:10 "Demas, in love with this present world, has deserted me . . ."
- James 4:8 "Draw near to God and he will draw near to you. Cleanse your hands, you sinners, and purify your hearts, you men of double mind."
- 1 Peter 5:8-9 "Be sober, be watchful. Your adversary the devil prowls around like a roaring lion, seeking someone to devour. Resist him, firm in your faith, knowing that the same experience of suffering is required of your brotherhood throughout the world."

So, who are you? Are you an embracer of worldly things that disappoint & fade, or are you aiming higher? Choose Jesus, He is Alive. Embrace Christ's salvation, value system, & personal integrity. Those things last & bring fulfillment. See also "What's in It For Me?" note 28.

* "All Hollywood corrupts, and absolute Hollywood corrupts absolutely." E.W. - American writer, Letters On Literature and Politics, Publisher; Farrar, Straus and Giroux, Oct. 17, 1977 pg. 302

167

DIVINE JUDGMENTS

Judgment is a complex matter & the scope of this short essay can only scratch the surface. There is a civil judgment which is serious as jail & the gallows. Then what I call "petty judgment" which is assessing others unfairly & w/o facts or mercy. It's not very serious - just petty. Then we have DIVINE JUDGMENT which is a Biblical matter & eternally serious. Now Divine Judgment has eight distinct divisions, but only five can be touched here*:

1. Judgment of the Cross – The world is condemned when Jesus Christ said "It is finished" John 19:30. M.F. Unger, a leading Bible scholar of the last century – "In the person of the Divine Substitute, the one who believes on Christ has been hauled to court, sentenced to condemnation and executed in the Person of his Substitute." John 5:24 (below)
2. Judgment of Believers – This is where "judgment begins in the house of the Lord." 1 Peter 4:17 The inspiration of the Apostle Paul explains it as Divine correction & chastisement. 1 Corinthians 11:31-32 (below)
3. Judgment Seat of Christ - Only for Christians & not about forgiven sins, but about their individual commitment, works & service. Eternal rewards or losses are involved. 2 Corinthians 5:10 (below)
4. Judgment of Angels - Fallen angels (demons) are eventual losers, even though many people embrace their desires, and serve them. See note 51 "Being Your Own Boss". But until the end of time we have to contend with their lies & schemes at every level. Jude 1:6 (below)
5. White Throne Judgment - Deals with eternal judgment of all unsaved of all ages. All who are not found in the "Book of Life" are cast into "the lake of fire". Rev 20:11 (below)

- John 5:24 "Truly, truly, I say to you, he who hears my word and believes him who sent me, has eternal life; he does not come into judgment, but has passed from death to life."
- 1 Corinthians 11:31-32 "But if we judged ourselves truly, we should not be judged. But when we are judged by the Lord, we are chastened so that we may not be condemned along with the world."
- 2 Corinthians 5:10 "For we must all appear before the judgment seat of Christ, so that each one may receive good or evil, according to what he has done in the body."

- James 2:13 "For judgment is without mercy to one who has shown no mercy; . . ." (Is this a reference to "petty judgment??)
- Jude 1:6 "And the angels that did not keep their own position but left their proper dwelling have been kept by him in eternal chains in the nether gloom until the judgment of the great day."
- Revelation 20:11 "Then I saw a great white throne and him who sat upon it; from his presence earth and sky fled away, and no place was found for them." (vs. 12-15 are intense also.)

I am grateful for the scholarship of M.F. Unger and others in the content of this sober subject. In the matter of judging others, which we all do (petty judgment), I would say "take the high road" - forgive & pray for those "thorny others" - don't judge & condemn them. That's God's business . . . In the matter of Divine Judgment, I would say be personally prepared – it's coming at all of us according to the Word of God. And there is a kind of judgment on sinners for walking contrary to God & neglecting his call while alive – see note 66 "The Blessing & The Curse". Choose Jesus, He is Alive. And be judged with the winning team.

* The other three are Judgment of Self, Judgment of Nations, and Judgment of Israel.

168

DEMON POSSESSION

We live in an advanced age where the university spirit says, "only what can be proven in laboratories is real" – that religious stuff is for losers." Of course, Hollywood plays with Demon Possession if it will sell. And they have made millions $ on "The Exorcist" & many others more recently. But is the concept of Demon Possession real? Many seasoned police officers or prison wardens will admit demon powers are real. My experience BEFORE coming to Christ has convinced me it's very real. (See note 43 "The Demon".)

I am amazed at the trends of today – teen suicides, mass shootings, dope epidemic, vehicle mass homicides, arson, etc. And with all the analysis & intellectual discussion, the possibility of demon action & possession is rarely if ever mentioned. Maybe it's considered a witch hunt, and in the center of the "crazy" category. Possibly the liberal media can't bear to identify with conservative Bible interpretations or anything Christian. At any rate, the powers of hell appear to be on the move and increasing. Demon Possession and activity seems to be all around us.

Some traits of the possessed: Hateful, overly proud, rude, profane, & arrogant. Anything said about Jesus is quickly back in your face. Most who resist their natural gender are oppressed or possessed. Bizarre actions, and resisting any authority may be D. P. I suspect folks who are subtle, devious, & plain evil in conduct. And there are polite intellectual demons that reject all vital Bible doctrines. I've known ministers who had a problem w/D. P. - see note #57 "Imposters". In Christ's day the Pharisees & Sadducees were religious leaders & had Him put to death. Take a look at John 8:44 to see their spiritual affiliation. In a nutshell, possessed folk "mess up" Godly truth & stability any way they can. My perspective on this subject comes from Scripture examples, personal revelations, AND 50 years plus interaction with people.

Of course, psychologically it would be explained that the collection of bad habits & traits in a person amount to a "demon." But I believe (from experience) that demons home in on the aroma of those bad habits & learned traits in a person, and magnify them. I believe also that demons can smell dope from a great distance & home in on it, same as sharks "smell" blood in the water & come rapidly after the victim.

Now even though Demon Possession is found in Old Testament & New Testament Scripture, often scoffers & liberals reject the concept as extreme literalism. They know that logically: IF D. P. is real, THEN Scripture is real, Jesus Christ is real, one-way salvation is real, Divine judgment is real, and heaven & hell are real. The problem with tossing the literal existence of demons is then all Scripture will be interpreted "loosie-goosie." See note 161 "Liberal Theology." I want to be AWARE of the spiritual environment around me - pondering Scripture gives light & helps to avoid darkness:

- John 10:10 "The thief comes only to steal and kill and destroy; I came that they may have life, and have it abundantly." Jesus Christ said that.
- Ephesians 2:1-2 "And you he made alive, when you were dead through the trespasses and sins in which you once walked, following the course of this world, following the prince of the power of the air, the spirit that is now at work in the sons of disobedience."
- Ephesians 6:12 "For we wrestle not against flesh and blood, but against principalities, against powers, against the rulers of the darkness of this world, against spiritual wickedness in high places."
- 1 Peter 5:8-9 "Be sober, be watchful. Your adversary the devil prowls around like a roaring lion, seeking someone to devour. Resist him, firm in your faith, . . ."
- James 4:7 "Submit yourselves therefore to God. Resist the devil and he will flee from you."

The references above speak loudly of the raging good vs. evil battle where our souls are at stake. Choose Jesus, He is Alive. His free salvation can be a matter of spiritual victory as Ephesians 6:10-20 explains clearly. See also note 160 "The Nature of Our Adversary".

169

FOUNDATIONS

Our first house we bought was in Lawton, Oklahoma & looked O.K., but later we learned it had no foundations. It had been hauled in & set on blocks – basically no continuous footings. Our second one was in Tempe, AZ and had been hauled in also & set on piers. Still no footings, but they did pour a concrete floor. It developed large cracks because in time the weight of the house pushed down the perimeter which in effect raised up the floor. We fixed/redeemed the problems, but it was a lot of work.

Biblical Christianity is a "house" & also has to have foundations – what it is based on. What is the groundwork - the basic, essential, primary factors, and at the bottom of the matter? Of course, the main foundation & cornerstone is Jesus Christ. Isaiah 28:16, 1 Corinthians 3:11. And is it an accident that Christ is called The Word – Greek "Logos", right at the start of the most dynamic Gospel of John?? 1:1 "In the beginning was the Word, and the Word was with God, and the Word was God." A prominent theologian, M. F. Unger said this; "Words are the vehicle for the revelation of the thoughts and intents of the mind to others. In the Person of the Incarnate Logos, God has made Himself fully known to man." And there is a profound union between Jesus Christ & the Scriptures.

Now the Scriptures are extremely important & amazing because THEY give the knowledge of Christ. And the god of this world (Lucifer) knows our knowledge of Jesus depends on a reliable Bible so he promotes liberal thinking on the veracity of Scriptures which can pull the rug from under Christianity. Is it any wonder that some colleges AND liberal seminaries undermine the Scriptures by attacking the authorship, date of writing, doctrines, and accuracy of the manuscripts? This G – note attempts to highlight some references on the excellence & Holiness of the written WORD:

- Exodus 24:4 "Moses wrote all the words of the Lord. . ." 1500 B.C.
- Psalms 12:6 "The words of the Lord are pure words: as silver tried in a furnace earth, purified seven times." 1000 B.C.
- Psalms 138:2 ". . . for thou hast magnified thy word above all thy name."
- Jeremiah 23:29 "Is not my word like fire, says the Lord, and like a hammer which breaks the rock in pieces?" 600 B.C.
- Matthew 4:4 "It is written, 'Man shall not live by bread alone, but by

every word that proceeds from the mouth of God.'" Jesus Christ said that.

- Luke 21:33 "Heaven and earth will pass away, but my words will not pass away."
- Hebrews 4:12-13 "For the word of God is living and active, sharper than any two-edged sword, piercing to the division of soul and spirit, of joints and marrow, and discerning the thoughts and intentions of the heart. And before him no creature is hidden, but all are open and laid bare to the eyes of him with whom we have to do."

There in that last reference is a hint of that profound union between Jesus Christ and the Scriptures. I had a glimpse of Jesus in a spiritual dream in 1977. He looked at me & said, "Learn of Me", which was positively the voice of God – (note 7 "I Saw the King"). Now those 3 words were a direct quote from the New Testament, Matthew 11:29. I believe (along with millions of others) that the Scriptures are the written WORD of God or Christ, and as a whole are the VOICE of Divinity to us humans. The people who bash the Bible are undermining their own prospects of peace and relationship with the Lord. How much better to build on revealed Truth as it is plainly given to us?? We all need "Foundations" to be complete as humans. Choose Jesus and His Word, they are Alive. See also note 65 "Why the Bible". Then for no extra charge, here's "a word" from Solomon – "He who gives heed to the word will prosper, and happy is he who trusts in the Lord." Proverbs 16:20.

170

COMMON LIES

This is an interesting planet especially considering how long & how many lies are out there. In this Gospel note I've tried to shine a light on only the most common:

- "What a pretty baby that is" . . . – When actually, you are thinking exactly the opposite.
- "We can run this stop sign, no one will notice." – Except that cop over there who needs one more citation for his shift quota.
- Have you ever been lost as a motorist and asked a local where is the hwy junction (or gas station, motel, grocery store, etc.), only to get deliberate false directions?
- "We can go to Mars . . ." – we're not only nationally broke, but why take on such an expensive & risky venture?? Weren't those 6 manned moon landings enough??
- "The race is to the swift" . . . There's at least one tortoise saying NO – (and Scripture, Ecclesiastes 9:11).
- "The earth is billions of years old." For Biblical truth & value system see AnswersinGenesis.org which cultivates Godly info that is more healthy for the SOUL.
- "I'll have lots of friends in hell." If so, the lost won't see them for the darkness, & they'll be too busy weeping & gnashing teeth to enjoy them anyway. Matthew 25:30

Well I believe in our modern world it is possible to feed on a lot of common lies & baloney. Especially with hundreds of TV channels w/NO commitment to truth & desperate for viewers to watch their sponsor's ads, which also have mainly a profit motive. Nothing needs to be said about Hollywood . . . "We are what we eat" and taking in false material will result in unhealthy & out of balance lives. People should realize that the most subtle lies will be on religious subjects such as Jesus Christ & the Word. We live in a spiritual battle (according to that Book), and our adversary has had thousands of years to perfect his best lies & strategies. Very likely the biggest lie is this one: "We don't need to be Born Again. As long as we are reasonably righteous God will accept us." Famous characters of history would condemn that lie real fast – especially the Old Testament prophet Isaiah & Jesus Christ himself.

- Isaiah 64:6 KJV "... all our righteousnesses are as filthy rags; and we all do fade as a leaf; and our iniquities, like the wind, have taken us away."
- John 3:3, 19 & 36 "Truly, truly, I say to you, unless one is born anew, he cannot see the kingdom of God. . . . And this is the judgment, that the light has come into the world, and men loved darkness rather than light, because their deeds were evil... He who believes in the Son has eternal life; he who does not obey the Son shall not see life, but the wrath of God rests upon him."
- John 10:1 & 9 "Truly, truly, I say to you, he who does not enter the sheepfold by the door but climbs in by another way, that man is a thief and a robber; . . .I am the door; if any one enters by me, he will be saved, and will go in and out and find pasture." Jesus said those things.
- 2 Corinthians 4:4 "the god of this world has blinded the minds of the unbelievers, to keep them from seeing the light of the gospel of the glory of Christ, who is the likeness of God."

Much more could be said on the subject of lies – common or rare ones. But the main questions are: "are the lies of this dark world & it's spirit taking me down?" –or- "Am I shielded from the devious curves that are thrown at me?" Psalm 84:11 "For the Lord God is a <u>sun and shield</u>; he bestows favor and honor. No good thing does the Lord withhold from those who walk uprightly." This includes perspective to beat the lies of this world. (Usually) Choose Jesus & His Word, THEY are REAL & they are Alive. See "Nature of Our Adversary" note 160 for the source of this world's lies.

171

INSPIRATION

This word has interesting meanings. It can be a matter of breathing in, as of air into the lungs. It can be an inspiring or being inspired naturally or emotionally, as by special people. Then we think of inspiring influences – any stimulus to creative thought or action. Typically, a sunrise, or a piece of art or music can "lift" or inspire our mood. Some similar words from a thesaurus are incentive, motivation, hearten, reassure, encourage, embolden, move, induce, prompt, fire, inflame, etc.

In Theology, inspiration is a Divine influence upon certain humans of history, as resulting in the writing of the Scriptures. And I find the Scriptures to be "Inspiring", and yes, fascinating too. Especially, as I grow older. Someone has said, "no one ever outgrows the Scriptures – The Book widens & deepens with our years," and gives more "inspiration". Now the concept of Inspiration of Scripture is immensely important. All evangelical Christian doctrines are derived from the Bible. A prominent theologian of the last century, L. Boettner referred to "Inspiration" as; "the mother and guardian of all other doctrines."[11] Is it any wonder that our adversary the devil works thru atheists & liberals to neutralize "inspiration," and lower the Bible to the level of just an ancient book?? I call this MAL inspiration . . . Another prominent theologian said, "In the small compass of God's Word there is stored more wisdom (and inspiration) that will stand the test of eternity, than all thinking done by man since his creation."[12] Arthur W Pink. Please let me offer some inspiring refs. from the Book:

- Psalms 19:1 "The heavens are telling the glory of God; and the firmament proclaims his handiwork."
- Psalms 12:6 "The promises of the Lord are promises that are pure, as silver refined in a furnace on the ground, purified seven times."
- Psalms 84:11 "The Lord God is a sun and shield: the Lord will give grace and glory: no good thing will he withhold from them that walk uprightly."
- Jeremiah 29:11 "I know the plans I have for you, says the Lord, plans for welfare and not for evil, to give you a future and a hope."
- Lamentations 3:25 "The Lord is good to those who wait for him, to the soul that seeks him."
- Matthew 4:4 "It is written, 'Man shall not live by bread alone, but by every word that proceeds from the mouth of God.'" Jesus said that.

- Luke 21:33 "Heaven and earth will pass away, but my words will not pass away." Jesus Christ
- Acts 20:32 "Now I commend you to God and to the word of his grace, which is able to build you up and to give you the inheritance among all those who are sanctified."
- Romans 15:4 "Whatever was written in former days was written for our instruction, that by steadfastness and by the encouragement of the Scriptures we might have hope."

The monks of Europe's monasteries from Egypt all the way north to Moscow, Russia are in the monastic way of life for Biblical/spiritual "inspiration". Their prayer mantra is <u>the Jesus prayer</u> – "Lord Jesus Christ, Son of God, have mercy on me, a sinner." I believe <u>that prayer</u> is the ESSENCE of saving faith in the whole Christian church, Catholic and Protestant, AND the key of Biblical "inspiration". Choose Jesus and His Word, They inspire. See also "Comfort from Above" note 136.

172

CATEGORIES

In February of '72 was my official date of commitment to Christ. The experience was real & amazing in many ways, and more interesting than I expected. I resolved at that time to study Christianity objectively at the source, to figure out what had happened to me. I studied the Book seriously for a few years, then began to memorize passages that stood out. It seemed logical to categorize the references. In my 5-6 years spontaneous (Holy Spirit led?) memory effort, I ingested nearly 900 passages in 84 categories. I have 7 larger categories of at least one typed page each which are: Sin, Error/Philosophy, Imposters, Inspiration, Comfort, New Covenant, & Jesus. The New Covenant category is the biggest, and the Jesus category is second biggest. I believe those 7 larger categories present a good "cross section" of the essence of Biblical Christianity.

Now for over 40 years I have reviewed from the references & categories daily. Probably the perspective of this gospel-note series is the "overflow ministry" of the memory work, and related Biblical studies. And I just noticed recently that I've already done at least one "note" on each of the top 7 categories: Sin-#137, Error/ Philosophy-#161, Imposters-#57, Inspiration-#171, Comfort-#136, New Covenant-#119 & 135, Jesus-#7 & 97 - The following list of Scriptures are the outstanding ones from each of the 7 categories above:

- Sin – "sin came into the world through one man and death through sin, and so death spread to all men because all men sinned," Romans 5:12 Sin has been a HUGE problem in this world – maybe the biggest of all.
- Error/Philosophy – "Beware lest any man spoil you through philosophy and vain deceit, after the tradition of men, after the rudiments of the world, and not after Christ." Colossians 2:8 KJV
- Imposters – "They say continually to those who despise the word of the Lord, 'It shall be well with you'; and to everyone who stubbornly follows his own heart, they say, 'No evil shall come upon you,'" Jeremiah 23:17 False teaching & leaders are a problem that goes back thousands of years.
- Inspiration – "For the Word of God is living and active, sharper than any two-edged sword, piercing to the division of soul and spirit, of joints and marrow, and discerning the thoughts and intentions of the

heart." Hebrews 4:12 The Word of God is Amazing!

- Comfort – "We know that in everything God works for good with those who love him, who are called according to his purpose." Romans 8:28
- New Covenant – "I will raise up for them a prophet like you from among their brethren; (Jesus Christ?) and I will put my words in his mouth, and he shall speak to them all that I command him. And whoever will not give heed to my words which he shall speak in my name, I myself will require it of him." Deuteronomy 18:18-19 God speaking to Moses 1500 B.C. & recorded by Divine dictation. Many other references of the beautiful New Covenant are in Old and New Testaments.
- JESUS – "Behold, I am laying in Zion for a foundation a stone, a tested stone, a precious cornerstone, of a sure foundation: 'He who believes will not be in haste.'" Isaiah 28:16 Prediction of Christ 700 years BEFORE the incarnation. Jesus Christ is the center of the New Covenant & the most premium revelation/miracle of God this old world has ever known. And the 4 Gospels clearly show that Jesus is sovereign over nature, Satan, sickness, and death.

In those few years of memorizing and arranging categories, I had no "plan" of the "special" groups above. They just happened, and I can truly see the cross section & essence of Biblical Christianity in the 7 choice "categories" above. It's not only what most protestant & catholic churches teach, but it's what I have discovered by experience that Christianity is all about. And the New Covenant really is God's final invitation to "dance" with Him.

Well it may have been easier w/less "homework" to just go with some "old line" denomination back then. But after 47 years of pursuing Jesus Christ & Scripture as per above, I'm 100% sure that choosing Jesus & His Word is the right track to receive God's blessing in this life, and a sure place in His eternal kingdom. See also note 28 "What's in It For Me".

173

STRONG DELUSION

To delude means to fool, as by false promises, wrong notions; mislead, deceive, or trick. Strong Delusion is a matter of being almost under a spell or trance of false thinking. I find it interesting that God Himself can inflict humans with this mental condition.

Possibly the most common reference to S.D. is in the second letter of the Apostle Paul to the Thessalonians which deals with the second coming of Christ. Strong Delusion is mentioned as a penalty at that future time for following a charismatic world leader called the "Anti-Christ" or "Man of Sin" who claims to be God, Chapter 2:1-11. But in a general sense, does Strong Delusion apply NOW?? The most famous Bible expositor of the last 300 years, Matthew Henry, had this to say: "He (God) will punish men for their unbelief, and for their dislike of the truth . . . He sometimes withdraws His grace from such . . . He gives them up to their own heart's lusts and leaves them to themselves." (M. H. – commentary on 2 Thessalonians 2:11) Scripture puts it this way; (and these refs. are 5:1 about the general sense of S.D.)

- Proverbs 1:24-26 "Because I have called and you refused to listen, have stretched out my hand and no one has heeded, and you have ignored all my counsel and would have none of my reproof, I also will laugh at your calamity; I will mock when panic strikes you,"
- Isaiah 66:3b-4 "These have chosen their own ways, and their soul delights in their abominations; I also will choose affliction for them, and bring their fears upon them; because, when I called, no one answered, when I spoke they did not listen; but they did what was evil in my eyes, and chose that in which I did not delight."
- Romans 1:21-22 "So they are without excuse; for although they knew God, they did not honor him as God or give thanks to him, but they became futile in their thinking and their senseless minds were darkened. Claiming to be wise, they became fools, "
- ** 2 Thessalonians 2:11 "Therefore God sends upon them a strong delusion, to make them believe what is false,"
- Hebrews 3:13 "But exhort one another every day, as long as it is called "today," that none of you may be hardened by the deceitfulness of sin."
- Revelation 22:11a "Let the evildoer still do evil, and the filthy still be filthy,"

Of course, a lifestyle of sin & avoiding God's call to salvation can bring Strong Delusion – NOW as well as during the dramatic events of Christ's second coming. But we also have intellectual denial of His call to salvation today. Many people are trusting in a liberal God, liberal interpretation of Scripture, good works/self-righteousness, universal salvation, New Age, personal achievements/status equating salvation, false religions, worship of science, etc. – anything but Jesus. They are offended by the "too narrow" one-way Jesus system – so they accumulate ARGUMENTS that support "anything goes" spirituality (even satanism), which all contradict Scripture & incurs STRONG DELUSION.

God has a real part in S.D. according to Scripture. People think God wouldn't do that . . . well all folks should do a good read of the Book to see what He has <u>already done</u> . . . making assumptions on the Nature of God may be real dangerous. We have Biblical accounts where <u>demons</u> were sent from God to be the agents of Strong Delusion. How about the case of Saul, 1 Samuel 16:23, the lying spirits in king Ahab's prophets 2 Chronicles 21-22, and Judas Luke 22:3. I have personally experienced demonic activity, & I know they can influence people's thinking & actions. See note 43 "The Demon".

Well, to finish I just say Strong Delusion is in the world today. The best defense against it is simply to choose Jesus & His salvation – they are Alive. Then cultivate that Faith. See also note 81 "The Commuter Flight", which deals with <u>light</u> from above. And that light is exactly the opposite of "Strong Delusion".

174

DIVINE DREAMS

This essay deals with the "picture shows" we get at night while sleeping. So, What are they? Why are they? Are they good for anything? A conservative Gospel lecturer/author named Ira Milligan has done a great job of analyzing the dream phenomenon. These are thoughts from his book "Understanding the Dreams You Dream", 2010 Destiny Image Publishers: ". . . Most dreams are indeed meaningful and helpful, although not all. (Dreams are) . . . God's most common method of communication. Elihu of Job (33:14-16) states that God gives us sealed instructions in the form of dreams . . . sealed (within parables) we seldom recognize them as being from God . . . The way God communicated with people most frequently in the Bible was through dreams. . . There is one obvious way of checking a dream to see if it is from God . . . messages are always consistent with His written Word." Milligan's book is a good read & is available thru Amazon.

The Bible has interesting refs. about dreams:

- Genesis 31:11 "Then the angel of God said to me in the dream, 'Jacob,' and I said, 'Here I am!'"
- Genesis 37:5 "Now Joseph had a dream, and when he told it to his brothers, they only hated him the more."
- Job 33:14-16 "For God speaks in one way, and in two, though man does not perceive it. In a dream, in a vision of the night, when deep sleep falls upon men, while they slumber on their beds, then he opens the ears of men, and terrifies them with warnings, "
- 1 Kings 3:5 "At Gibeon the Lord appeared to Solomon in a dream by night; and God said, 'Ask what I shall give you.'"
- Joel 2:28 "And it shall come to pass afterward, that I will pour out my spirit on all flesh; your sons and your daughters shall prophesy, your old men shall dream dreams, and your young men shall see visions."
- Matthew 1:19-20 ". . . her husband Joseph, . . . resolved to divorce her quietly. But as he considered this, behold, an angel of the Lord appeared to him in a dream, saying, 'Joseph, son of David, do not fear to take Mary your wife, for that which is conceived in her is of the Holy Spirit;"
- Matthew 2:12 "And being warned in a dream not to return to Herod, they departed to their own country by another way."

There's lots more Scripture refs. on dreams ALL of which are revealing of God's communication with people. I do not know why in our day folks generally put little "stock" in their dreams and don't look for God's message. I have received <u>much</u> useful info from mine - some <u>before</u> the "born again" event of Feb '72. In addition to my "lucid" spiritual/religious content dreams, (which have been amazing), God has given practical help & guidance in dreams to me. And the messages were clear, and to the point. I've lost a few to time & memory, but at least these six remain:

- "The big one" for me was a vivid dream of Jesus Christ – (See "I Saw the King" note 7)
- Revelation of spiritual character – extreme liberal associate in ministry exposed in a dream to be possessed w/the wrong spirit. (see "Imposters" note 57)
- Confirmation of major life/job change – I "saw" associates in ministry D.H. & B.S. in a dream 2-3 days before meeting them. (see "The Chaplains" note 70)
- Correction of dangerous path – God can get a graphic message to us in dreams using a similar or symbolic disaster scene that applies, and He did.
- Closure on failed romance – long lost love can be settled in a personal & discreet manner by Divine dream, and it was.
- The blessing of God – grape vines in 3 rows in front yard of a previous home of ours – beautiful clusters of green-blue large grapes.

Well this essay can only "scratch the surface" of Divine Dreams. But I should say that "Seeking God" and being open to FAITH & Divine Guidance may easily bring value to one's dreams. And my personal Born-Again experience really seemed to activate dream communication with God. It's sad that so many folks neglect something that's free & useful . . . Choose Jesus, He is Alive. Connect with a package of benefits this old world knows nothing about. See "What's in It For Me" note 28.

175

TOUGH TO BELIEVE*

The Bible does have many tough & hard to believe teachings. Now I don't claim to have all the answers, neither do I know all the questions. But the teachings below are some that just challenge the mind & appear to be most incredible to many normal folks:

- 6-day creation - Science today is about unanimous on theories of the deep time origin of this planet.
- Noah's flood, then fire from the sky on Sodom & Gomorrah as judgments.
- Virgin birth of Jesus Christ - I've heard atheists refer to this tough teaching & all Christian doctrine as "immaculate deception". "Their condemnation is just." Romans3:8)
- Resurrection & ascension to heaven of Jesus Christ
- Heaven & HELL
- Strong Delusion - God blocking folks after they frustrate Him too much & too long (see S.D. note 173)
- Rapture of saved believers, then 2nd coming of Jesus Christ at the end.

Many people refuse to intellectually commit to the above for fear of ridicule, rejection, etc. and wax liberal with friends & colleagues, then create alternate interpretations/philosophies that forsake most Bible doctrine and the Lord Himself. But maybe God has put hard to believe material in the Book <u>as an affiliation test</u> or screening device? (He does test people. . .) At any rate, I personally believe <u>my best chance</u> of being in good standing with the Author of the Book is by just accepting it as it is. I lose nothing in this life (except a few false friends), and if those "Tough To Believe" teachings are "spot on" or not, my identifying w/them should be a credit to me at my judgment. And it's easier for me to believe the Biblical accounts than the big bang & deep time theories of atheists. Our world is not balanced in a space orbit around the sun, mostly covered w/water, & abounding w/marine, plant, & animal LIFE by a grand accident.

While most of the above T.T.B. are "bold as a lion", <u>in our day</u> we are mostly dealing with a <u>hidden God</u> that requires FAITH to find Him. The contrast between the active/aggressive Bible accounts, and the hidden God concept is also a blocker for many. We must SEEK God by accepting the T.T.B. (<u>which includes</u> repent, pray through, baptism, attend church,

& gather arguments FOR belief, etc.) Then the Nature of God can be seen in those tough teachings we find in the Bible from cover to cover. And He is the kind of Character that can and does give more faith, hope, life victory, healing, guidance, perspective, etc... But some folks build their own gallows by gathering false arguments & sin, then stubbornly living w/ backs to God. See note 66 "The Blessing and The Curse".

- 2 Chronicles 15:2b "The Lord is with you, while you are with him. If you seek him, he will be found by you, but if you forsake him, he will forsake you." (I believe this is an early hint of "Strong Delusion".)
- Psalms 77:11 "I will call to mind the deeds of the Lord; yea, I will remember thy wonders of old."
- Isaiah 45:15 "Truly, thou art a God who hidest thyself, O God of Israel, the Savior."
- Matthew 11:29 "Take my yoke upon you and learn from me; for I am gentle and lowly in heart, and you will find rest for your souls." Jesus Christ (The hidden God concept is seen in the above 2 refs.)
- Acts 17:26-27 "And he made from one every nation of men to live on all the face of the earth, having determined allotted periods and the boundaries of their habitation, that they should seek God, in the hope that they might feel after him and find him."
- Hebrews 3:12 "Take care, brethren, lest there be in any of you an evil, unbelieving heart, leading you to fall away from the living God."

From the beginning of the Bible record it has been a challenge for some to believe God's "Tough Teachings". So, it is in our day. In my case, as soon as I decided to just "deal with it", God began to reveal the rewards of FAITH. And as I faced God and the teachings of the Book, His presence & blessing became more clear in my life. I write "Gospel notes" to share the good news. Have you connected?? "Behold, I stand at the door and knock; if anyone hears my voice and opens the door, I will come in to him and eat with him, and he with me." Jesus, Revelation 3:20 Choose Jesus, He is Alive. See also "Why The Bible?" note 65.

*Besides T.T.B. Teachings, there are "Tough To LIVE" Teachings which may be the greater challenge. See note #178.

176

TALE OF TWO STEVES

In one of the earlier Gospel-notes of this series, we have a striking contrast between two Apostles of Christ – that's in note 25. In this "G-note" note 176, we have a striking contrast between a couple of my relatives. Now they were BOTH special & dear to me. But they illustrate the extremes in the American family – one "churched", and the other not "churched".

My uncle Steve was an Air Force veteran who married in the church, then continued in family church activity with his wife & kids till the end of his life in 2014 – Steve was 85. He had a successful marriage, successful career, good home life & long retirement in Sun City, AZ. More or less the picture of God's blessing in suburbia, USA.

My nephew Steve (another family) was from a dysfunctional "nest" & was not a veteran. He was not oriented towards the church or religion, and his family & marriage was mostly without light or discipline from above. He had a "gypsy spirit" and was in trouble with the law from an early age. Jail time, then spotty employment. This cycle went on for decades, then sadly at age 44 Steve was shot in a gunfight with the police. The cop my nephew shot survived, but Steve didn't. Dramatically the picture of living without God's blessing in suburbia, USA.

I am amazed at the contrast between the two Steves above, and I don't know why there is so much other diversity in the family I was born into. Unless God wanted me to see all kinds of lifestyle extremes or contortions -- positive & negative, rich & poor, conservative & liberal, etc., then write gospel conclusions. And my take on the bigger picture of our society & its failures is the basic family unit is collapsing. From the 50's, television has become more & more devoid of truth & decency (the god of this world has mostly taken it). Prayer has been removed from public school. Bible plaques have been removed from the court. Most mothers have gone to work leaving kids at home alone too much. Alcohol & drugs are stylish. The Christian life has been lampooned & lambasted in our schools & universities. Then science & technology is seen as the final answer. We have had perfect "soil" for a secular & faithless society for decades. We are now seeing the outgrowth of all that liberalism, and the resulting hate & sin & violence & killing all around. The question is, CAN WE GET STABILITY BACK??

I want to believe there is hope in the U.S. & world today BECAUSE of the Balance of Nature. (see note 92) The pattern of history is "the pendulum swings". We have had serious issues & decline for decades, but God is not dead! I would like to believe people are ready to bring back salvation & church affiliation -- even if it's not politically correct! I look forward to a season of church growth & better family pictures. But it has to start w/the individual. Are YOU ready to move toward a relationship w/ God? Are YOU ready to experience God's blessing & freedom in Christ? Here's a few refs. from God's Word that seem to fit this essay:

- Psalms 37:25 "I have been young, and now am old; yet I have not seen the righteous forsaken or his children begging bread." (I can vouch for the truth of this, and also say it's better to be righteous than "riot"eous in lifestyle. . .)
- John 14:6 "Jesus said to him, 'I am the way, and the truth, and the life; no one comes to the Father, but by me.'"
- Romans 10:9 "if you confess with your lips that Jesus is Lord and believe in your heart that God raised him from the dead, you will be saved."
- Romans 12:2 "Do not be conformed to this world but be transformed by the renewal of your mind, that you may prove what is the will of God, what is good and acceptable and perfect."
- Galatians 6:7 "Do not be deceived; God is not mocked, for whatever a man sows, that he will also reap."

I could have gone the way of my nephew Steve above – I came from a more hopeless district in Phoenix. But I heard the Gospel of Christ & responded, which has been much more than I expected. My wife & I have 47 years of that Blessing & Hope to reflect back on. And Regeneration in Christ is available to "whosoever will". Choose Jesus, He is Alive. See also "The Blessing & the Curse" note 66.

177

RULES OF THE GAME

In most any game the object by standard logic is to WIN, and not LOSE. And many in competition, besides following the "Rules of the Game", actively reach out of themselves to draw on a higher power. (Dallas Cowboys praying before game, some folks rub a lucky charm, some chant a magic phrase like win, win, win, etc.) And besides the rules & reaching out of oneself, we all need a strategy & resolve to WIN. Here's a few common attitudes of winners AND losers.

WINNER	LOSER
Always part of the answer.	Always part of the problem.
Always has a plan.	Always has an excuse.
Sees an answer for all problems.	Sees a problem in all answers.
Says, "It may be tough, but it's possible."	Says, "It's too difficult."
Says, "Let me do it for you."	Says, "That's not my job."

Now it's counterproductive for athletes to eat unhealthy, not exercise, do drugs & alcohol, no discipline, NO RULES, bash head against a wall for entertainment (I have seen this), then expect to win – WIN WHAT??

In the game of life it's counterproductive to absorb false information, not exercise oneself in TRUTH, go for psychology, & extreme yoga, no discipline or seeking the real God, liberalism, bash head against Jesus Christ (deny His deity & glory), then expect to win – WIN WHAT??

So, what are the "Rules of the Game" of life if we want to really WIN?? 1) Acknowledge God – give the Bible of history some respect. It's God's "rule book" & the BEST statement of TRUTH of all time. 2) Receive God's salvation. That is Jesus Christ which is the message of both Old & New Testaments. 3) Absorb the truth of the ages. While the Decalogue & the whole Bible deals with Divine taboos & truth, three brief works of Solomon are loaded with interesting & practical RULES of wisdom, folly, & love. Those works are Proverbs, Ecclesiastes, and Song of Solomon. Now Solomon was supposed to be the wisest of the wise of all time. 1 Kings 3:12. Read his works to see why . . .

So, what is the BENEFIT or PRIZE of WINNING?? It's a matter of finding peace with God and living that way. Minimizing sin & life dominating bad habits. Walking in light & finding the best version of ourselves. Finding our niche of productivity so we can enjoy our labor & benefit from it. Being useful to our family, employer, state, & country. It's a matter of promoting good health by diet & lifestyle, and generally getting Blessed. Then to inherit the "pie in the sky" (heaven for eternity) which is a mighty fine pie!

- 2 Chronicles 34:1-3 "Josiah was eight years old when he began to reign, . . . in the eighth year of his reign, while he was yet a boy, he began to seek the God of David his father;" (The best "Rule of the Game" is seeking God early BEFORE we are entrenched in worldliness & "Strong Delusion", note 173)
- Proverbs 8:17b "Those who seek me diligently find me."
- Psalms 119:105 "Thy word is a lamp to my feet and a light to my path."
- John 8:12 "Jesus spoke to them saying, 'I am the light of the world; he who follows me will not walk in darkness, but will have the light of life.'"
- Matthew 22:14 "For many are called, but few are chosen."
- 1 Corinthians 9:27 "I pommel my body and subdue it, lest after preaching to others I myself should be disqualified." Paul the apostle.

The Bible presents the "Rules of the Game" from cover to cover. It gives examples & principles of winners & losers of all sorts. And Jesus Christ said there would only be a "few" that WIN. Be on the winning team. Choose Jesus, He is Alive. Romans 10:9 "If you confess with your lips that Jesus is Lord and believe in your heart that God raised him from the dead, you will be saved." And the Church is there to help us live the Christian life & be blessed. See also "Set Yourself Up", note 20.

178

TOUGH TO LIVE

In another Gospel Note the theme is "Tough To Believe". That's a look at hard to believe teachings of Biblical Christianity (note 175). This "G-note" deals with the greater challenge of just living the Christian life. Most will admit the believing part is easy. The following "stuff" is why many folks don't continue in the faith & church involvement:

From the gospel of Luke we have a discourse of Jesus that teaches his followers to "love their enemies", "bless those who curse you & pray for them", no vengeance & "turn the other cheek". Then "give to all who beg", "lend to others expecting nothing back", and "don't judge others but forgive them". Luke 6:27-37 We have another world's assessment of our values in Luke 16 where Christ says, "what is exalted among men is an abomination in God's sight". Verse 15

From the book of Romans chapter 12 we are told "Do not be conformed to this world but be transformed by the renewal of your mind, that you may prove what is the will of God, . . ." v.2. That chapter goes on to service in the church like teaching, contributing the tithe, giving aid, acts of mercy, etc. And of course, the New Testament never cancelled the Big 10 – no idols, no blasphemy, no lies, no neglecting the Lord's day, no adultery, don't kill thy neighbor, etc. etc. And all of this may be easy compared to MARTYRDOM which may be a part of it during the great tribulation – Revelation 12:11. (We should keep in mind that from the garden beginning, GOD TESTS US . . .)

Now what about Christ's word in Matthew 11, "Take my yoke upon you . . . for my yoke is easy & my burden is light?" Is there a contradiction here? From my own experience of living the "life" for 47 years there's no contradiction, and here is WHY: When we repent of sin & accept Christ, we join the "family" of God. Being Born Again/regenerated is a work of the Holy Spirit, and that Spirit empowers us to live "the life". We won't be perfect, but God looks at our sincerity & resolve. I realized early on it might be "Tough To Live" this new lifestyle, but God showed me a few miracles (note 33), His presence (note 73), His guidance (note 143), and His appointments (note 151). My faith held up and increased.

Sure, it may be a challenge to live God's way, but it's doable. Engaging in a denomination with all its specific doctrines, traditions, ritual, preaching, social mixing, etc. can be helpful. But all that doesn't "float in the air" – it has to be based on something. Besides solid doctrinal teaching, that something is personal decision/determination, personal prayer, personal Bible reading, personal relationship w/Jesus Christ. Without those PERSONAL elements the Christian life is TOUGH TO LIVE, & our landscape is littered w/folks who have given up on the Church AND Jesus. If we want vitality in our spiritual life – if we want our "cup" to "runneth over" (Psalms 23), we need to get that personal stuff right.

Well I don't find God's Book & way of life to be that "Tough to Believe" or "Tough to Live". I find it to be very interesting & satisfying knowing that the true purpose of life is unfolding around me. But I had to start somewhere & that was way back when I heard & responded to the Gospel. Christ's call is still in the world today because "Jesus Christ is the same yesterday, and today, and forever." And "Behold, I stand at the door and knock; if any one hears my voice and opens the door, I will come in to him and eat with him, and he with me." Hebrews 13:8, Revelation 3:20 Choose Jesus, He is Alive. See also note 28 "What's in It For Me?"

179

<u>THE RESURRECTION</u>

From the beginning of the world death has been a HUGE problem. Death is bleak & permanent. For thousands of years early man was generally ignorant of such a notion as "the resurrection". Egyptians about 2400 B.C. seemed to believe in an afterlife. The very rich ones made pyramids to protect & house their mummies & possessions in the hope of a resurrection. About that time our Bible began to be written, & the resurrection is mentioned by Job. (Job is considered by many to be the oldest part of Scripture.) He writes ". . . after my skin is destroyed, this I know, that in my flesh I shall see God." 19:26 Then about 800 B.C. we have an excellent glimpse of resurrection when a dead man was thrown into Elisha's tomb on top of his bones. The dead man came back to life. 2 Kings 13:21 And there are other allusions of Old Testament resurrection.

Well, it appears to me that "the resurrection" is <u>the most powerful teaching</u> of the Bible BECAUSE it applies to ALL MORTALS – if it's real we can beat <u>death</u>. And for those who want to believe in "the resurrection", Jesus Christ the Jewish Messiah came along 2 K years ago & gave us the CLEAREST information on this glorious subject. He brought back <u>at least five</u> persons during His three-year ministry in Palestine. When Christ raised Lazarus he gave these words, "I am the resurrection and the life; he who believes in me, though he die, yet shall he live, and whoever lives and believes in me shall never die. Do you believe this?" John 11:25-26 And that penetrating question, "do you believe this," has rattled millions of people for thousands of years.

One of the first <u>rattled</u> by the resurrection of Jesus Christ was none other than "doubting" Thomas <u>the apostle</u>. The other 10 had seen the resurrected Jesus on His day of emerging alive from the tomb. Thomas was missing & when told they had seen Jesus alive, he said ". . . I will not believe." Eight days later he ate those words when Christ appeared to the 11 together. Jesus zeroed in on Thomas & said, ". . . see my hands; and put out your hand and place it in my side; do not be faithless but believing." Thomas answered, "My Lord and my God!" That response of Thomas the realist always gives me a thrill.

In spite of the Thomas incident, the resurrection may still be hard to believe. BUT we do have the yearly & global Easter holiday. Is it just an illusion or grand scale religious deception?? I don't think a fake Easter event could change the world & hold up for 2K years. Logically we really can "believe this", and when we do "believe w/o seeing", God has promised to bless us. see John 20:24-29. The Resurrection and Eternal Life is not only God's best gift to this troubled world, but it is also the main message of Christianity.

- Isaiah 26:19 "Thy dead shall live, their bodies shall rise. O dwellers in the dust, awake and sing for joy! . . ."
- Daniel 12:2 "And many of those who sleep in the dust of the earth shall awake, some to everlasting life, and some to shame and everlasting contempt."
- 1 Corinthians 15:21-22 "For as by a man came death, by a man has come also the resurrection of the dead. For as in Adam all die, so also in Christ shall all be made alive."
- 1 Corinthians 15:55 "O death, where is thy victory? O death, where is thy sting?"

The New Testament teaches that once we believe in Christ & the Resurrection, we can personally participate in it. And that should be a comforting thought for all who will ultimately meet the coroner & undertaker, which includes YOU, and ME . . . Choose Jesus, He is Alive. Romans 10:9 "If you confess with your lips that Jesus is Lord and believe in your heart that God raised him from the dead, you will be saved." See also note 163 "To Be Or Not To Be".

180

PRINCIPLES OF FAITH

People who respond to the Gospel and cultivate Christian Faith gradually or sooner learn that God exists. They "see" this in spite of ALL the atheistic talk to the contrary. He also speaks to us in various ways – especially the written WORD. And this amounts to a personal relationship. With "eyes" of Faith we know we have that personal relationship. We know God can hear & answer even silent prayer. And we can "see" the absence of faith in ourselves & others – that natural worldly rhythm around us. Listed below are some Principles of Faith that may be helpful:

P - Exercising Faith causes it to grow. Listening to the Gospel is crucial. Romans 10:17

P - Faith will be rewarded by God. And our giving to the cause will return to us. See note 30.

P - People who discover the WORD will learn that it is the MOTHER LODE of Faith & divine truth.

P - Little Faith will be honored. It's no excuse to say, "I don't have faith like that . . ."

P - Prayer in the name of Jesus is a wonderful privilege, and close to being "magic". Sadly, too many never discover it. See note 37 "What is Prayer?"

P - Faith can be squashed by unbelief. Some folks accumulate arguments why they don't believe, then when they should pray about a need or crisis they back away. They can lose their soul too.

P - Faith & organized denominations & cults are not necessarily the same. Many denominations have procedures & traditions that contradict Scripture & squash Faith. Especially liberal denominations.

P - Some religious/church people have no Faith or are blinded to it by unbelief (& or) hypocrisy.

P - Faith is most useful outside church because that is where the real world is. See "Which Church is Right?" note 49.

P – Faith and Christian values will incur censure from lost people.

- 2 Timothy 3:12-13 "Indeed all who desire to live a godly life in Christ Jesus will be persecuted, while evil men and impostors will go on from bad to worse, deceivers and deceived." Persecution from the worldly spirit is truly a negative principal of faith. It is probably the #1 reason why new believers often re-think their decision & commitments to God.

- Hebrews 11:1-3, & 6 "Now faith is the assurance of things hoped for, the conviction of things not seen. For by it the men of old received divine approval. By faith we understand that the world was created by the word of God, so that what is seen was made out of things which do not appear... And without faith it is impossible to please him. For whoever would draw near to God must believe that he exists and that he rewards those who seek him." All of this chapter is the finest review of Faith in the Bible. The author is unknown, but most think Paul or Apollos wrote it – by Divine inspiration.

Without Faith we are all pirates in God's eyes, destined to gravitate away from Him. And of course, that crowd will go out of its way to assassinate Christian Faith – especially today. However, that is only to be expected since the purest Man of Faith – Jesus Christ was executed for His perfect Faith walk. We are fortunate because we can now receive Christ's Spirit & Faith through the Gospel, and be shielded from some of the persecution that has buffeted believers before us. (See Psalms 91, Proverbs 30:5-6, Ephesians 6:16). And being aware of the principles & elements of Christian Faith can make living "in Christ" a little easier (or a lot). Choose Jesus, He is Alive. "If you confess with your lips that Jesus is Lord and believe in your heart that God raised him from the dead, you will be saved." Romans 10:9 See also "Faith" note 75.

181

BARGAINING WITH GOD

Bargaining with God is a bold act of faith that is practiced by folks that are in straits of some sort. Of course, the first reality in BWG is the confidence/assurance that God exists & can deliver the "goods" that we need. Today God's Biblical character & dominion is not commonly accepted due to liberal & atheistic trends. Well, not because of my exceptional faith or righteousness, years ago I did some BWG & He came through for me. I've done some since then also. But I haven't been alone in this – below are other examples of this bold & maybe sometimes reckless spiritual venture.

When I was in High School a friend & neighbor T. Scott had a daughter my age who came down with cancer. T. Scott prayed & told God he would accept Christianity & live for God if God would heal his daughter. The healing happened. The best story is of an Air Force serviceman in the early 80's who encountered a newborn Korean infant in a So. Korean civil clinic. He prayed that God would allow him & his wife to adopt the baby girl. After substantial S.K. red tape & U.S. military procedures, and getting the serious adoption fee in cash, his locker was robbed the day before the adoption finalized. He prayed again that God would give him enough poker winnings that night to replace the stolen cash, and if so, he would raise the girl right, and not gamble any more. The money came back in a flash, the adoption went through, the baby girl grew up to be an A. F. medical officer, then became a civilian dental technician, & my hygienist for the last 6-8 years. And she is among the best.

A classic example of BWG in the Bible is Hannah in 1 Samuel 1. She was "to be" the mother of Samuel but was barren for years. She bargained w/God that she would give the baby back to God if He would allow her to conceive. God delivered "the goods", & Hannah kept her side of the deal. She gave the toddler Samuel to the temple & priest Eli. Amazing & touching story of faith.

Another classic story is King Hezekiah of Judah – 2 Kings 20:1-6. This man came down with a lethal sickness & Bargained with God to heal him for his past righteousness. God heard & delivered the healing & gave Hezekiah 15 more years of life.

- Ecclesiastes 5:4-5 "When you vow a vow to God, do not delay paying it; for he has no pleasure in fools. Pay what you vow. It is better that you should not vow than that you should vow and not pay."

- Matthew 7:7-8 "Ask, and it will be given you; seek and you will find; knock, and it will be opened to you. For everyone who asks receives, and he who seeks finds, and to him who knocks it will be opened." Jesus the Christ said that.
- Philippians 4:6 "Be careful for nothing; but in everything by prayer and supplication with thanksgiving let your requests be made known unto God."
- ** Hebrews 11:6 "But without faith it is impossible to please him: for he that cometh to God must believe that he is, and that he is a rewarder of them that diligently seek him."
- 1 Peter 5:7 "Cast all your anxieties on him, for he cares about you."

Bargaining (or reasoning) with God is a matter of reaching out in faith to a personal God, asking/expecting something to happen personally. And that is what Christianity is all about. We are fortunate to have a God who is big enough, and able & willing to act on our behalf. (We are also fortunate to have God's Word the Bible which explains all this in great detail . . .) Too many religions in our day expect God to be way out there, & not involved personally in our lives. What good is that?? Without a personal relationship with God, most faiths reduce down to a popularity contest/ social club. But I like the notion of a close relationship – and maybe an occasional bold "Bargaining With God". It all starts with believing "that he is, and that he is a rewarder of them that diligently seek him." ** Choose Jesus & His salvation. They are ALIVE. See also "Reasoning With God", note 68.

182

HUMAN NATURE

This is a broad subject, & a glimpse at humanism could shed some light. That is a focus on the attitudes & interests of man or mankind, having the qualities of a man. And it can imply godless characteristics such as egotism, arrogance, irreverence, sacrilege, self-dignity, vanity, stateliness, etc. This Gospel Note seeks to present a few common Human Nature traits to ponder:

- Human Nature says, "Me first." At what age does this begin? How about 1 minute old . . .
- H.N. says, "My dog (or anything of mine for that matter) is better than yours."
- H.N. is contrary & says, "Anything YOU like (or value, respect, cherish) I (or WE) DON'T."
- H.N. justifies itself & says, "I'm O.K., but YOU are NOT O.K."
- H.N. typically lies its way out of any kind of trouble from the beginning of time.
- H.N. loves to complain & disagree. Thousands of years ago Moses ran into this with the early Israelites. He said to God something like this, "kill me at once, I can't deal with these people . . ." Numbers 11:10–15.
- H.N. likes power for itself, & dominating others (the more the merrier) is just a bonus. The Book says, "you shall receive power when the Holy Spirit comes upon you . . ." Acts 1:8 This is a God approved kind of power.
- H.N. typically has a weak (or dead) conscience. A Jewish Rabbi I admire wrote "Human Nature rarely condemns what we really want." Daniel Lapin. Consider the religious Pharisees & Sadducees that condemned Christ, also things like the Spanish Inquisition, the Nazi Holocaust, then today we have Islamic fundamentalist murder & mayhem.
- H.N. moves in on the benefactor or potential customer w/lots of charm & personality. But after getting what it wants there's indifference, distance, & typically no reciprocation – see Amnon & Tamar 2 Samuel 13
- Philosophically H.N. says, I AM. "I AM" was a primary revelation of God's character to Moses about 3500 years ago. Exodus 3:14 For man to go with "I AM" is a pride trip & amounts to horrible rebellion against God. See note 45.
- Life is a matter of give & take. But with H.N. it's mostly "take". Christ came along 2 thousand years ago to offer man a giving nature thru the Gospel, but it's optional & often neglected. 2 Peter 1:4.

Well, most theologians strongly agree that Human Nature (and humanism) clearly proved its darkness when man's religious & political systems condemned & executed the Messiah Jesus Christ, who was God in the flesh visiting His planet. And it's a sure thing that we are in trouble with God, & need the Divine ointments of regeneration, justification, grace, etc. (see note 119 "Meat in The Soup"). Now the Virgin Birth of Jesus Christ is an essential doctrine of Biblical Christianity. It means that Christ can (and did) change humanity for the better precisely because He was 100% SHORT of man's Nature. I was told recently by a liberal Catholic nun that "Jesus was just a man!" But how could He visit this planet & improve Human Nature (and the world) if He was "just a man"?? And how could he infuse into "whosoever will" the contrasting traits of meekness, modesty, courtesy, ambition, spirituality, healing, righteousness, faith, holiness, humility, etc. if He was "just a man"?? Here's a few refs. from The Book on the NATURE of "the first man" Adam who represents our fallen race, & the NATURE of "the second man" Jesus Christ who represents HOPE:

- Ecclesiastes 9:3b "The hearts of men are full of evil, and madness is in their hearts while they live, and after that they go to the dead." (Adam)
- Jeremiah 17:9 "The heart is deceitful above all things, and desperately corrupt; who can understand it?" (Adam)
- 1 Corinthians 15:47-49 "The first man was from the earth, a man of dust; the second man is from heaven. As was the man of dust, so are those who are of the dust; and as is the man of heaven, so are those who are of heaven. Just as we have borne the image of the man of dust, we shall (let us) also bear the image of the man of heaven."
- Romans 12:2 "Be transformed by the renewal of your mind, that you may prove what is the will of God, what is good and acceptable and perfect."

Human Nature is truly a bucket of slime, & God clearly condemns it in Scripture. The things fallen human nature needs most to elevate it are BIBLICAL TRUTH and FAITH. We can choose to embrace H.N. – OR – we can choose God's FAITH solution. That is accepting Christ's free salvation, then cultivating that relationship. See "Serving God", note 9. When we allow Christ to regenerate & transform us, a new life & nature truly begins. "O ye who would enter the glorious rest; And sing with the ransomed the song of the blest; The life everlasting, if ye would obtain, ye must be born again." Anon. Choose Jesus & His Nature. They are Alive and well, in spite of hell, and Human Nature. See also "Religious Human Nature" note 183.

183

RELIGIOUS HUMAN NATURE

I've heard it said that humans have a deep religious instinct which is common to all. This amounts to "Religious Human Nature". And, "most people have some sort of religion. (At least they know which church they're staying away from." LOL, John Erskine) This Gospel Note will touch some charming aspects of our religious nature that the previous "note" left out.

- It is "Religious Human Nature" to say, "I am RIGHT, you're NOT."
- It's R.H.N. that says proudly, "We believe whatever we want to believe, and we do not need any rational or legitimate basis for our belief system."
- R.H.N. <u>invents</u> its own gods & says, "I (we) don't need no Bible or Jesus either."
- R.H.N. will swallow a big lie such as polygamy and make a taboo of a small issue like drinking coffee or tea. Jesus said something about "straining out a gnat & swallowing a camel." (Matthew 23:24 – all of that chapter speaks loudly of false religion.)
- R.H.N. gathers arguments to support false beliefs instead of studying the WORD for answers. We should use <u>the Scriptures</u> instead of flimsy man-made proofs of false doctrine. "Study to show thyself approved . . ." 2 Timothy 2:15
- R.H.N. replaces God's <u>revealed</u> standard of righteousness (John 3:16, 36) with self works such as community service or animal rescue, etc., etc. See "I Don't Eat Pork" note 155.
- It's R.H.N. to over emphasize miniscule issues such as the <u>right</u> day of worship or the <u>right</u> style of baptism or the <u>right</u> diet w/o meat, etc. Then ignore vital issues like the Lordship of Christ & His Atonement, Authority of Scripture, etc.
- R.H.N.: "I am popular in my social circle, & these are decent church people – I must be right w/God."
- It's R.H.N. to say of <u>one's faith or denomination</u>, "THIS is THE PLACE to find God – those other churches are a waste of time.

The New Testament reveals to us that many people "have a form of Godliness w/o the power thereof". <u>2 Timothy 3:5</u> That has to be a subtle ref. to "Religious Human Nature". – Playing all kinds of social & religious games w/God w/out really connecting. And R.H.N. can be eternally misleading when Jesus Christ at judgment time may say, "I never knew you", Matthew 7:21-23. The place to find legitimate spiritual vitality is in one's decision & determination & commitment. This amounts to praying thru, if we focus that "prayer" into Biblical truth & the Salvation of Jesus. Afterwards "Divine Presence" (note 73) can be felt. Prayer becomes more natural & spontaneous, "about everything", Philippians 4:6 ("What is Prayer?" note 37) And God answers, which is a matter of having substance & depth in our faith – not just the veneer of R.H.N.

Well, I believe our "Religious Human Nature" is a subtle bucket of slime. We all need to "beat the system" by accepting Christ's free salvation, then cultivating that relationship. (See "Serving God", note 9.) When we allow Christ to regenerate & transform us, a new life & nature truly begins. "O ye who would enter the glorious rest; And sing with the ransomed the song of the blest; The life everlasting, if ye would obtain, ye must be born again." Anon. Choose Jesus & His Nature. They are Alive and well, in spite of hell, and R.H.N.

184

IS HELL FOR REAL?

This should be a serious question for all mortals who eventually cease to live. When we die, then what? Heaven, Nothingness, or Hell? To prove there is a negative afterlife one needs to either crack it open & take certified pics. - or die & go there. So, for all practical purposes, a place like Hell has to be proven logically.

1. Common sense & nature screams for justice. Should characters like Herod, Nero, Stalin, Hitler, Charles Manson, etc. just cease to exist w/out punishment for their evil & murders? If there is a living & just God, he has to punish sin & rejection of conscience at all levels.
2. One of the most convincing & logical proofs of Hell is the experience of a cardiologist named Maurice Rawlings. This guy was a pioneer of CPR & some of his patients he recovered from clinical heart stop death came back terrorized by a temporary encounter with Hell. Their stories are intense! "Beyond Death's Door" 1978, available thru Amazon. He also wrote "To Hell and Back" 1993.
3. For those who accept the Scriptures as the Word of God, it can be viewed as logical proof. And the concept of Hell is very consistent in Old Testament and New Testament. The O.T. Hebrew word for Hell is Sheol, which is the sorrowful place of the dead. The N.T. Greek word for hell is Hades. Scripture teaches that Sheol & Hades are a holding place for unrighteous dead till the final judgment. There is a very revealing "picture" of Hades in the Gospel of Luke chapter 16. Christ himself gives the case of a rich man who died & was, "in anguish in this flame." The dialog in this afterlife account is amazing. Then we have Scofield theologians reflecting on it. "Luke 16:23-24 shows that the lost in Hades are conscious, possess full use of their faculties, memory, etc., and are in torment. This continues until the final judgment . . . and Hades itself, will be cast into the lake of fire." (Revelation 20)
4. Broadly speaking, if Jesus Christ was God in the flesh (and Scripture clearly teaches this), then his rejection & brutal murder by humanity calls for God's wrath in the form of severe punishment of the unrepentant. Why not a hell? (And a curse on the way there. - see "Blessing & Curse" note 66.) I could add more logical arguments for hell, but space is short in this essay.

A subtle problem today is to undermine Scripture by assigning extreme doctrine (and miracles) to mythology. And if we eradicate a literal Hell from the Book by liberal interpretation, what else goes?? I have been amazed to learn that many so called "Christian" believers reject nearly ALL the main doctrines of the Bible. This grossly disrespects God's Holy Book, and how can they expect to BENEFIT from those glorious teachings?? Hell is the only one that is bad news. Now do I agree w/the concept of Hell? Not especially, but if God put me here to seek Him, it's not right for me to weasel to the left & dismiss doctrine I dislike as many folks do. It's God's teaching not mine. And we are not the first to face God's justice. Some 2800 years ago Israel & it's king Zedekiah were judged & punished on the large scale as a nation, and below is a summary of WHY. Then realize that we do the same on the small scale as individuals because we too are humans. (see "Human Nature" notes 182 & 183)

- 2 Chronicles 36:13 & 16 ". . . stiff neck & hardened hearts, . . . mocking the messengers of God, despising his words, and scoffing at his prophets, till the wrath of the Lord rose . . ."
- Psalms 9:17 "The wicked shall depart to Sheol, all the nations that forget God."
- Matthew 13:41-42 "The Son of man will send his angels, and they will gather out of his kingdom all causes of sin and all evildoers, and throw them into the furnace of fire; there men will weep and gnash their teeth." Jesus C. said that.
- Mark 9:48 "Where their worm does not die, and the fire is not quenched." Jesus C. said that.
- Revelation 20:15 "and if any one's name was not found written in the book of life, he was thrown into the lake of fire."

If we can trust the Book to be authentic and accurate as God's contract to humans, then Hell should be very seriously avoided. I was born & raised in Phoenix AZ & personally spent enough time in a hot place. I figure the salvation of Jesus Christ is the best fire insurance policy around – unless He lied . . . Choose Jesus, He is Alive. See also "Crowded Cities" note 5 and "Why Literal?" note 74.

185

DRAGONS OF THE MIND

It appears that each one of us has 3 lives – our Social life goes on at work, school, church, etc. Our Private life is in our home. Then we have our Secret life which goes on in our head – thoughts, desires, ideas, etc. Now dragons are mythical creatures which don't actually exist – or do they??

I believe dragons exist and live quite well in our thought or Secret life. Our brains replay & review positive AND negative events, comments, personal actions, etc. maybe hundreds of times (or more). Then bad feelings & memories can be magnified greatly becoming "Dragons" blowing smoke. (Some folks would call them worries.) These dark shadows (?) typically take the joy & peace away from people and produce depression, stress, paranoia, greatly exaggerated issues, character assassinations, heartburn, etc. Dragons GROW, then come between people, and they feed well on regrets, misunderstandings, jealousy & hate. I am sure a lot of today's mayhem, murders, suicides, etc. are due to psychotic powers of the mind & memory running wild. I am also sure that sensitive souls have the greatest problem with "Dragons of the Mind". Then it's a sure thing that families & churches can be destroyed by those dragons.

Now the most logical purpose of life is to live & die happy. Bob Marley summed it up with his famous phrase, "Don't worry, be happy." But it's not going to happen with "Dragons" blowing smoke on us 24-7. Christian people should pray for the power to ignore & forget undesirable & negative recordings of the memory. We have the privilege of prayer – why not use it?? (See also note 37 "What is Prayer?") God's people should also practice the forgiveness Christ recommended in the Lord's Prayer – Matthew 6:12. (See also note 35 "Freedom in Forgiveness") Someone said that, "Forgiveness is like setting a prisoner free, and finding out that prisoner is YOU." Anon. These two actions go a long way towards killing those "Dragons of the Mind". A lot of people think the "power" to kill "dragons" and be happy is from their "debominations" & social clubs. Bob Marley & associates thought it comes from the smoke of cannabis. Some think alcohol does the trick. I believe the power is in personal application of Apostolic principles – especially prayer & forgiveness.

God's people should realize that we live in a raging spiritual battle, and a lot of it goes on between our ears. Thought control is essential if we want the victory in Christ. (See also "Mindset of Victory" note 103.) And thought control is a challenge for all. I have personally had better control of my "dragons" when I pray for the "power" to resist them – Every time there seems to be a problem. Scripture sheds light on this important issue:

- Psalm 94:19 "When the cares of my heart are many, thy consolations cheer my soul."
- John 1:12 KJV "But as many as received him, to them gave He power to become the sons of God, even to them that believe on his name."
- Romans 8:31 KJV "If God be for us, who (or what) can be against us?" (Our "dragons" dump on us ONLY if we like it AND allow it.)
- Philippians 4:6 "Have no anxiety about anything, but in everything by prayer and supplication with thanksgiving let your requests be made known to God."
- Philippians 4:8 "Whatever is true, whatever is honorable, whatever is just, whatever is pure, whatever is lovely, whatever is gracious, if there is anything worthy of praise, think about these things."
- 2 Timothy 1:7 "For God did not give us a spirit of timidity but a spirit of power and love and self-control."

I believe demons of hell have the power to influence some of our thinking. They are amused when we develop bad thought patterns, knowing we can access Holy Spirit power to block their schemes. 2 Corinthians 10:3-5. I personally want to live happy & die laughing as did the old man (Dick Van Dyke) in the classic Disney flic "Mary Poppins". Biblical principles may be the surest way. Choose Jesus, He is Alive. See also note 136 "Comfort From Above".

186

HOMELESS VALUE SYSTEM

A value system is a person's set of ideals. What is held in respect and honor – those things that are good and important & desirable. Like self discipline, knowledge, work, money management, and faith. But there have always been folks who are homeless or headed in that direction. So, what is their "Value System"?

A "Homeless Value system" will typically not have the self discipline element. Time is not valued and is wasted. Priorities are out of order which causes more time to be wasted, see "Obsessions" note 61. Gaining knowledge is not important here, neither is schooling since many homeless are unteachable. Hosea 4:6 "My people are destroyed for lack of knowledge; . . ." Work is low in the value system along with accountability & responsibility. And excuses are numerous why work is impossible. Money management is VERY difficult due to the compromised earning power (as per above), AND bad habits which cling tightly such as alcohol, drugs, other vices, etc. There will not be much faith in a Homeless Value System because typical stabilizing influences like family, teachers, priest/minister, Bible, etc. are not important or just outright despised.

In addition to the above distorted values, it seems that the H.V.S. encourages "eating" persons close by such as parents, children, close friends, relatives, etc. A case of note is a young man who rubbed his wealthy stepfather the wrong way for several years. In another case the only son at age 50 or so pulled a shotgun on his father & sisters to show just who was "the big one" in the family. Both cases ended up excluded from the will where substantial inheritance was distributed. And the typical H.V.S. outcome may not be as extreme, but homeless values do cause folks to gravitate down to a sad "picture". A "Homeless Value System" can be seen as a lifestyle of cultivating "BAD LUCK". But there is good news – God's salvation & blessing is REAL and can be seen as a lifestyle of cultivating "GOOD LUCK".

Now the Gospel means GOOD NEWS. Christ's salvation puts sin behind us and regenerates our mind so we can look up & receive good things from above. Then Christ's touch brings access to a new power – "to all who received him, who believed in his name, he gave power . . ." John 1:12 It also brings order & structure into our lives. Salvation brings more healthy influences. Preaching & fellowship with like-minded souls promotes a new orientation of values. And the Gospel means affiliation with Divine things. Such as Presence 73, Healing 132, Guidance 143, & Priorities 156 – all of which dissolve the Homeless Value System, and replace it with direction, purpose, and HOPE. We not only have a much better chance of being successful & "home-ful"?, (notes 83 & 106), but salvation also gives a premium "home" in eternity.

- "He who tills his land will have plenty of bread, but he who follows worthless pursuits will have plenty of poverty. Proverbs 28:19
- "He who gives heed to the word will prosper, and happy is he who trusts in the Lord." Proverbs 16:20
- "Woe to those who call evil good and good evil, who put darkness for light and light for darkness, . . . Woe to those who are wise in their own eyes, and shrewd in their own sight!" Isaiah 5:20-21
- "Seek first his kingdom and his righteousness, and all these things shall be yours as well." Matthew 6:33
- "Do not be conformed to this world but be transformed by the renewal of your mind, that you may prove what is the will of God, what is good and acceptable and perfect." Romans 12:2

For a winning morning prayer each day try this one, - "Lord Jesus Christ Son of God, have mercy on me a sinner, and help me to redeem the time today." <u>That</u> is Choosing Jesus and His Value System, which are <u>Alive</u>. They grease the gears of life and promote a whole gang of premium benefits ("What's in It For Me" note 28). Prosperity is quite often a part of it.

187

THE POPULARITY CONTEST*

This American political system & society is set up as a popularity contest. We choose our leaders because we like them. Then our Hollywood entertainers rise to the top because of popularity. There is a pattern here which also appears even in High School - the "in crowd" & popularity circle. Then many places of employment have an inner circle where position & advancement have much to do with social vibrations. Wherever there is a Popularity Contest, the code is: Image = Credibility = Prestige, without which contestants (?) are or feel like one legged football players.

Now there are people who are Socially Awkward & have trouble with image, credibility, & prestige. They distrust other people & crowds from their early years and despise popularity contests. They say & do the wrong things at the wrong time, and they ask the wrong questions. Then their own awkwardness & distrust of others grows to where they have pessimism & depression in any social group. These people often hear the Gospel of Christ and gravitate into a fellowship center - the Christian Church (which is supposed to be a hospital for sin-sick humanity). But many good hearted & genuine believers have no social grace, and they typically find that churches prefer the socially graceful & adjusted. Socially Awkward souls typically feel unwelcome & don't continue long in a church. Many resort to Sun. AM religious TV programs to satisfy their spiritual needs.

So, what is the solution to this problem? I believe awareness itself is a good start. If we know it's a common problem for many, there's comfort right there - us S.A.'s are not alone. Also, our focus has to be on Christ & His Word - not social vibrations. If we have Jesus Christ in our heart, the social stuff will take care of itself. (If not, we are not out much.) Another solution is to keep looking for the right church fit. A prayer for Divine Guidance can be huge here (see notes 49 & 143).

I write this Gospel Note as a Born Again REALIST who has 47 years (or more) of inside observation & experience with the church & this problem. The Christian value system & church TRULY does have the power to lift people from sin & humanness, but "The Popularity Contest"/ social club (& related issues) can really turn off prospective members. I believe the typical church group would have more attendance if the socially awkward were better received, and that church group would have a better portion of the Spirit of Christ & love.

Some Scripture refs. that may apply:

- 1 Samuel 16:7 ". . .The Lord sees not as man sees; man looks on the outward appearance, but the Lord looks on the heart."
- Proverbs 18:24 "There are friends who pretend to be friends, but there is a friend who sticks closer than a brother." (That "friend" is none other than Jesus Christ.)
- Psalms 62:5-6 "For God alone my soul waits in silence, for my hope is from him. He only is my rock and my salvation, my fortress; I shall not be shaken."
- John 1:11 "He came to his own home, and his own people received him not." (Now the Lord was not "Socially Awkward" as such, but Christ was <u>not</u> well "received" by the established church of His day. And me & my Gospel-notes have been "stiff armed" by churches with a P.C./ social gospel emphasis.)
- John 13:34-35 "A new commandment I give to you, that you love one another; even as I have loved you, that you also love one another. By this all men will know that you are my disciples, if you have love for one another." Jesus said that.

The point of this Gospel message is just this: We can ALL look to the Lord & His program & be blessed. But if there is a BLOCKER (which comes in many forms), we need to deal with it carefully <u>before</u> it ruins our faith. ABIDING in Christ and His Word in tough times carries us through. Choose Jesus, He is Alive. "Rejoice always, pray constantly, give thanks in all circumstances; . . ." 1 Thessalonians 5:16-18 See also "Comfort From Above" note 136.

* "Am I mad, to see what others do not see, or are they mad who are responsible for all that I am seeing?" Leo Tolstoy

188

OTHER GODS

In today's world it appears to be sophisticated to believe in "Other Gods" or Polytheism. Maybe it's broad-minded & friendly to accept other religions & gods. Certainly, it's politically correct to be at least respectful of "Other Gods." And there is a popular phrase that says, "Travel is fatal to prejudice, bigotry, and narrow mindedness." (Mark Twain) This mindset says basically that other gods are GOOD.

In ancient Biblical times there were about 41 "Other Gods". At the time of Christ there were about 20 Greek gods. Today Hinduism has a staggering 33 million gods. Considering the quantity & diversity of "gods" recognized today, it's admittedly tough to make a stand for "one God & one way". And there is a popular culture today which frowns on anyone who dares to claim allegiance to Biblical concepts – they think us believers cannot be intelligent beyond the moron I.Q. level . . .

Well, if the Bible is valid, then it is a HUGE gift of light from above telling who God is & how us sinful humans can connect w/Him & be blessed all the way to Heaven. And the "Other Gods" question was answered quite early in history – Moses received the 10 Commandments in a dramatic way about 1500 B.C. (See Exodus 20). That choice revelation of God & His rules addresses "Other Gods" #1 on the Decalogue list. Idols are #2. And God reveals right there that He is a jealous God. Israel learned the hard way in the next 3400 years that God punishes the dis-loyal. See Exodus 20:5 & 34:14. This is Biblical & world history – And this planet would be TOTALLY different if Israel had not violated Commandments #1 & #2. How many pogroms against the Jews (& the Nazi holocaust) have happened in those 3400 years? Their population & land area would be EXPONENTIAL to what it now is. The earth would now look like what is in prophecy for the Millennial Kingdom of Christ after the 2nd Coming. See Micah 4:1-4, & Zechariah 14:8-9.

Now again, if the Bible is valid, as soon as I admit "Other gods" exist, I tear down the Bible & insult God. This is simple logic. And if Commandment #1 flows from the mind of God, & the majority of the world's population is entangled with millions of "Other Gods" (& idols), wouldn't it suggest how LOST this planet is IN GOD'S EYES?? I know it would not be politically correct to call "Other Gods" and faiths FALSE, but

Scripture does exactly that. If spiritual light is what we want, the below refs. may be useful to ponder:

- Exodus 20:3 "You shall have no other gods before me."
- Deuteronomy 4:35 "To you it was shown, that you might know that the Lord is God; there is no other besides him." (Moses addressing the Israelites 1500 B.C.)
- Psalms 16:4a "Those who choose another god multiply their sorrows;"
- Psalms 81:8b-9 "O Israel, if you would but listen to me! There shall be no strange god among you; you shall not bow down to a foreign god."
- Romans 1:18 "For the wrath of God is revealed from heaven against all ungodliness and wickedness of men who by their wickedness suppress the truth." (Going after "Other Gods" is implied in this.)
- 1 John 4:1 "Beloved, do not believe every spirit, but test the spirits to see whether they are of God; for many false prophets have gone out into the world."

On the subject of "Other Gods" I would ask, what do they have to offer? This in effect was asked by an Old Testament prophet named Elijah. There was an awesome Biblical SHOWDOWN revealing the POWER of Israel's "One" God & false gods. That incident involved the false god Ba'al & his 450 prophets. They lost badly (1 Kings 18:17-40). In our day I have been amazed with the "Born Again" relationship w/the same "One" God. He has shown me "neat" stuff also - to confirm my faith & commitment, (which is "Why I Write" Gospel Notes. See note 158) Choose Jesus, He is Alive. The Biblical Trinity is real – in the long run "Other Gods" don't stand a chance. See "New Age" & "The Steam Roller" notes 56 & 102.

189

TURNING THE CLOCK BACK

How fine it would be to have a time machine with a clock on it for returning to a certain point in the past. We could go back & change decisions & mistakes that have been disastrous & troublesome. We might go back a week, a month, a year, maybe a decade or two. Then we could fix the mistakes & re-live those months & years without the horrible consequences of our past misdeeds. I could change some real regretful junk, and YOU probably could too. Of course, "Turning the Clock Back" is a fantasy. But let's get our "money's worth" and extend this fantasy to one who is dead.

My nephew Steve recently was killed by the police in Glendale, AZ for a bold mistake he made – (note 176). If he was not saved and now in hell, I'm sure he would say, "Let me go back to 1 year before the gunfight. I could get my life in better order and avoid the disaster of catching a police bullet." If my nephew was saved and presently in Heaven, he would probably say, "Keep your time machine – I'll stay right here in this wonderful place – why go back to that crazy sin drenched planet & it's curse."

Now of course we can't go back, and one English novelist, Aldous Huxley was negative about even learning from our mistakes: "That men do not learn very much from the lessons of history is the most important of all the lessons that history has to teach."[13] BUT I WOULD LIKE TO BELIEVE that we can learn from our sins & mistakes IF we look to God for forgiveness of those "dumb strokes". If we "draw near to God, He will draw near to you (us)." James 4:8 And if we live close to Jesus Christ as Scripture suggests, God's Blessing will be a big part of our life. Considering that shield (Psalms 91) & package of benefits like Divine Presence 73, Divine Guidance 143, Divine Appointments 151, etc. we won't have as much need to fantasize about changing the past. We'll get a lot of it right the first time. Now Perfection should be a goal, but British P.M. James Callaghan offered this, "You never reach the promised land. But you can march toward it."[14] And "marching toward it" with God's help is what living the Christian life is all about.

Psalms 16:11 "Thou dost show me the path of life; in thy presence there is fullness of joy, in thy right hand are pleasures for evermore." 73:24 "Thou dost guide me with thy counsel, and afterward thou wilt receive me to glory." Proverbs 4:18 "But the path of the righteous is like the light of dawn, which shines brighter and brighter until full day." Jeremiah 29:11 "For I know the plans I have for you, says the Lord, plans for welfare and not for evil, to give you a future and a hope." Romans 8:28 "We know that in everything God works for good with those who love him, who are called according to his purpose." 2 Corinthians 6:2 ". . .Behold, now is the acceptable time; behold, now is the day of salvation."

A time machine is truly a fantasy; but receiving the Gospel of Jesus is Biblical truth. Why not get started on that New life & Path today? Why accumulate excess mistakes & regrets & consequences of sin when we can get in on God's Blessing. "Therefore, if anyone is in Christ, he is a new creation; the old has passed away, behold, the new has come." 2 Corinthians 5:17 Choose Jesus, He is Alive. See also "The Blessing & the Curse" note 66.

190

ON THE JOB REFLECTIONS

On the Book of Job that is . . . Now this excellent but mysterious part of Scripture is considered by many to be the oldest part. And it deals with maybe the oldest problem in the world, "Why is this happening to me??" All ask this when tragedy strikes. The problem is we may not have a good answer, or anyone else. (Except God . . .) My mother mentioned Job early in my childhood – she had a serious handicap. I think she may have concluded that life has questions & problems that rattle us to the BONE.

The book in a nutshell – Job was at the top of his society & very rich & righteous. Had a wonderful family. We see a Sovereign God in a heavenly council where "sons of god" (Angels) were present, and Satan comes in. Our adversary challenges God to strike Job as a test & God signs off on the plan. Then tragedy by surprise struck Job down. First all his possessions were destroyed or stolen, then all his children & workers killed. Then he comes down with a terrible skin problem & boils. Three comforters come to Job who only accuse Job of secret sins & don't have real answers. Then a fourth comforter (Elihu) enters with a better argument/speech that Job was being cleansed by God. Unger - "Elihu adds a momentous truth that affliction of the righteous is disciplinary." Then God answers "from the whirlwind" & gives His authoritative speech. Job is humbled & justified by God. Then God doubles Job's blessing & gives him 10 more children & 140 more years.

Now Job's ancient society was considered to be about 2100-1900 B.C. – the time of Abraham. Scofield gives this – "the patriarchal period is inferred from his great age, various geographical references . . . and no mention of the law & the Tabernacle . . . lofty Biblical concepts of God, man, Satan, righteousness, redemption and resurrection may show . . . the wide extent of revelation in that region even before Scripture." And for the mystery, "there is no answer except the attitude of worship in which we humbly acknowledge that a Sovereign God cannot be required by men to give all the reasons for what He chooses to do." (God has the Divine Counsels, we must have the FAITH.)

Some key refs in Job – there are plenty more but I must be brief. . .

- 1:7 KJV "The Lord said unto Satan, 'Whence comest thou?' Then Satan answered the Lord, and said 'From going to and fro in the earth, and from walking up and down in it."

- 13:15 “Though he slay me, yet will I trust in him: but I will maintain mine own ways before him.”
- 19:25-26 KJV “For I know that my redeemer liveth, and that he shall stand at the latter day upon the earth: And though after my skin worms destroy this body, yet in my flesh shall I see God:”
- 23:10 KJV “But he knoweth the way that I take; when he hath tried me, I shall come forth as gold.”
- 42:5-6 KJV “I have heard of thee by the hearing of the ear, but now mine eye seeth thee. Wherefore I abhor myself, and repent in dust and ashes.”
- Proverbs 18:24 “There are friends who pretend to be friends, but there is a friend who sticks closer than a brother.”
- John 10:10 KJV “The thief cometh not, but for to steal, and to kill, and to destroy: I am come that they might have life, and have it more abundantly.” (Jesus said that about 2000 years after Job's life & trials.)

I would dare to say the first & last 2 chapters of the book of Job are so excellent that Scripture would not be complete w/o them. And it's interesting that Job said a lot of harsh things in the chapters in between about God, but God seems to have taken it as a friend. Job argued with his friend God, who was big & noble enough to settle the problem and still be Job's friend. God's graceful nature & character is revealed. Now in the New Testament we have almost a parallel story of a “suffering victim” by the name of Lazarus. He was well off in a prominent family w/Christ as a personal friend. I believe this Gospel account goes a few levels above the Job account because Lazarus even dies, but Jesus went to his tomb & called him out. That is resurrection from the dead! John 11:1-44 And it's a fabulous picture of OUR better day & age with complete Scripture & with Jesus Christ as personal friend & advocate. See John 15:13-17

Well I finish this by saying the Book of Job and ALL Scripture is CHOICE because it shows IF God is involved in our life, we are Blessed & ultimately WIN BIG because He is good & He takes care of His friends. Are YOU on His team? Are YOU His friend?? Choose Jesus, He is Alive. See also “Comfort From Above” & “Divine Healing” notes 136 & 132

191

THE BIG LIE

Hitler said, "If you tell a lie big enough and keep repeating it, people will eventually come to believe it. . ."[15] Well, in our modern scientific age we have a whole world of people who accept Charles Darwin's theories of evolution & origins of life as fact. For over a hundred years those evolution theories have swept the world, & even permeated the Christian church. But there are some conservative thinkers who consider evolution to be "The Big Lie."

Few people realize that when C. Darwin was dying in England, he denied his own theory; . . . sitting up in bed . . . a look of agony came over his face as he said, "I was a young man with uninformed ideas, I threw out queries, suggestions, wondering all the time . . . To my astonishment the ideas (of evolution) took like wildfire. People made a religion of them." Afterwards he asked Lady Hope, a hospice friend, to preach to his other friends about; "Christ Jesus . . . and His Salvation. Is not that the best theme?" C. Darwin - from Voices from the Edge of Eternity, 1968, 2012 pgs. 245-246

Our god of this world adversary (Lucifer) knew, 1) long before Darwin that "monkeying" with origins in Genesis destroys the need for a Savior from sin. If there was no created Adam & Eve, and no fall into sin, then logically we need no Christ & His bloody atonement. Our adversary also knew, 2) that mythical interpretation of Genesis compromises ALL Scripture – it's anybody's guess what the rest of it means, if anything. Without the Genesis historical origin & fall into sin, logically we need NO Church or its doctrines – which is where we are today in academia. (And they teach our kids to question our Biblical faith and value system.) Our adversary also knew, 3) that humans by nature are BIASED against God and WANT to believe a fundamental LIE which releases them from the rules (10 Commandments, Christ's words, etc.), and the authority of God.

Now ultimately evolution is a RELIGION based on FAITH because no one was there - not even a scientist . . . So, the question of creation or evolution boils down to; do we WANT to believe God & Creation (there is plenty evidence – see www.answersingenesis.org *). And Abe Lincoln said, "That Book we should take as it is written & where we can't take it by reason, take it by faith."[16] - OR – do we WANT to reject God & have faith (& religion) in Darwin's theories? It appears that today's proud humans typically do not WANT to believe the Bible & WEALTH of evidence for creation. They have said "evolution is a light on facts." (The American Biology Teacher, Vol 35 pg. 129). Jesus Christ said, "I am the light of the world; he that followeth me shall not walk in darkness, but shall have the light of life." John 8:12 KJV

- Psalms 11: 3 "If the foundations be destroyed, what can the righteous do?"
- Proverbs 19:21 "Cease my son, to hear the instruction that causeth to err from the words of knowledge."
- John 5:46-47 "For had ye believed Moses, ye would have believed me; for he wrote of me. But if ye believe not his writings, how shall ye believe my words?" Jesus said that.
- Romans 1:18, 20 "For the wrath of God is revealed from heaven against all ungodliness and unrighteousness of men, who hold the truth in unrighteousness. For the invisible things of him from the creation of the world are clearly seen, being understood by the things that are made, even his eternal power and Godhead; so that they are without excuse."

So, what difference does it make? Well today's generation have confidence in Darwinism & stay away from God's "hospital for sin sick humanity" - the Christian Church. Many are adamant & hate the idea of religion – especially Christianity. Especially the latest youth culture . . . And the fruit of sin is increasing in the world. Look at the increase in crime, abortion, divorce, odd marriage concepts, family dysfunction & mayhem, mass murders, political riots, etc... The world is falling apart at the seams.

Well, I believe God specializes in baffling & humbling the MINDS of men. (He zapped me – see "My Miracles" note 33). He could have taken millions of years to create the world & life, but to do it in six days just shows how great He is. He could have done it in six hours. I believe God wants us to make a stand for the WORD, not undermine it by accepting atheistic theories. And Jesus Christ made it clear that believers are blessed & go to an eternal heaven. Creation/Christ rejecters set themselves up for "Divine Judgments" (see note167). To any evolutionist I ask; Are you saved, is your soul fireproof? See notes 39 & 184, "What is Saved?", and "Is Hell for Real?" Choose Jesus, He is Alive. And THAT is no LIE.

* answersingenesis.org – Answers in Genesis, Ken Ham & associates have been challenging the Christian church with its Biblical origins with NUMEROUS books on the subject & even has a Creation Museum, also a FULL SIZE replica of Noah's Arc in north Kentucky, USA.

192

<u>NON-TRADITIONAL</u>

The word tradition brings to mind standard or usual things. Maybe traits & habits of some culture. This Gospel-note takes a look at <u>Non-Traditional Ministries</u>. We are all familiar with regular ministries - the church & it's minister, priests, & missionaries, etc. But the non-traditional are not as obvious or recognized – even among religious people. The following list is by no means complete.

- We met a NTM character in Eugene, Oregon over forty years ago that found his calling giving a biology laboratory class to home schooled H.S. kids. He is creationist & presents the option that God created the world & life rather than the evolutionary theories as fact. Steve is qualified to teach the class & has done it over 40 years for free.
- We met another character who found his niche of NTM giving Bibles near and far. He works hard for his money then gives much of it away through Bible placement. John's ministry is not affiliated with the Gideons – he is a kind of "lone ranger".
- Prison ministry - visiting jail birds with comforting words & prayer/ befriending.
- One church we attended years ago had a wealthy couple who would give financial help to needy folks on an incognito, "off the record" basis. But they got <u>our attention</u> by giving my wife & I an SUV at a time we really needed one. That was a REAL surprise and seriously "good news" if not the gospel, and we were not too proud to take it – we put nearly 80 thousand miles on it.
- We have been on several cruise ships to find a Bible study/meeting on sea days (when ship is not in port). On this ship a couple have been leading the class & claim to have this NTM. They appear to be in their niche and are doing a good job.
- I believe the military chaplaincy is a NTM. I fell into it after Viet Nam & it changed my life. Those chaplains were good men & I learned a lot about the ministry. See note 70 "The Chaplains". The last one was a classic in that he went thru seminary with <u>no desire to preach</u>. He just wanted to be a Police Chaplain & did extra study on the subject of suicide. John is a very interesting character.
- I have been writing "Gospel-notes" for forty years and only recently

realized this is a Non-Traditional Ministry. Slow learner, I guess.

- An Australian on this ship told us about a Thailand based NTM he was affiliated with. It's a rescue home for Thai orphans who have been exploited for pedophile sex. I don't know how Gospel oriented the ministry is, but it appears to be 100% legitimate as a Non-Traditional Ministry.
- I really shouldn't throw in the case of the Catholic nun that cared for about 75 stray cats. But I will. She was authorized by the convent to do cat rescue - apparently because she was so liberal, she could do little damage to human souls as long as she was occupied with spiritually worthless cats.
- Then we have the food ministry. Usually the pastor "visits" local supermarkets & loads up on date expired groceries. Church side-rooms are stocked & needy folks can help themselves. (Church mice love food ministries . . .)

Most theologians believe the traditional Christian church started with the commission from the resurrected Jesus Christ we find in Matthew 28:19 "Go ye therefore, and teach all nations, baptizing them in the name of the Father, and of the Son, and of the Holy Ghost." Shortly afterwards the early church & churches began to form, along with the traditional role of the minister/priest. But many people cannot or will not be reached by "traditional" means. Non-Traditional Ministries like those above help to "fill in the gaps". And I have found that God is VERY capable & will have a witness when & where He wants one to be. He can get the message of Christ to those who need and want that message. (Elijah got a "message" even from wild ravens – maybe not gospel, but it was an early food ministry - LOL?) "The ravens brought him bread and meat in the morning, and bread and meat in the evening; and he drank of the brook." 1 Kings 17:6

I suppose the whole concept of ministry is a mystery & farce to some folks. And indeed, Scripture bears this out. The "street-wise" apostle Paul wrote to the Corinthians, "the message of the cross is folly to those who are perishing, but to those who are being saved it is the power of God." 1 Corinthians 1:18 About 49 years ago I was typically "perishing" in my sin & Christ rejecting lifestyle. A non-traditional ministry was there for me. My hope is that others will find Christ by whatever means the gospel message is promoted. Choose Jesus, He is Alive. See also "Why I Write" note 158.

193

THE ARABIAN CONNECTION

We recently spent some time in Dubai, which is east of Saudi Arabia. We were impressed with the clean & safe & modern city. There seemed to be good economics & hospitality. We would go back there. I was given a copy of the Quran & I have been reading it. Now Dubai is not far from Mecca & Medina, the origins of Islam some 1400 years ago. And there has been tremendous worldwide growth of this Arabic religion in that time – it now dominates at least 42 countries in Asia, Europe, and Africa w/much more than a billion members. And Islam has many good-hearted folks like Cornelius of Apostolic times – "a devout man who feared God with all his household . . ." Acts 10:2.

I am intrigued with Islam for the reasons above, but I look at an ancient bad politics root which causes "a fly in the ointment". That root goes back about 2600 years before Muhammad wrote the Quran. In Genesis chapter 15 we have the PROMISE of numerous descendants to Abraham (the Israel nation). In the next chapter we have Abraham's lack of PATIENCE waiting for the promised son, by promoting heirs thru a slave woman, Hagar his wife's maid. Ishmael was born illegit. & prophesied in that chapter to be ". . .against every man and every man's hand against him". While God did say he would "greatly multiply (Hagar's) descendants . . ." Genesis 16:10-12, Isaac the promised son was born fourteen years later to Abraham's wife Sarah as per Genesis 21:1-5. (why the delay??) This "bad family root" explains why Arabs & Israel grew apart & have bad political – who likes who - differences to this day. And Muhammad promoted stark refusals of history & Scripture, which he surely had access to in his day.

Islam accepts the first 5 books of Scripture & the Psalms as do the Jews. They also recognize the "Injil" (Gospel) of Jesus. But of course, the Quran is Allah's final word which does contradict the basic fabric of Jewish & Christian teaching. The ancient bad politics root shines thru. The supposed angelic author of the Quran – Gabriel -- would not contradict Old & New Testament Scripture. But Lucifer would contradict that Scripture – artfully at that. And I do admire the literary style of the Quran. But there is no Biblical record that "Abraham & Ishmael were laying the foundations of the House" – as Quran 2:127 suggests.

Their #1 pillar of faith is "no God but Allah . . ." Well that squashes the Trinity – Father, Son, & Holy Spirit – Three in One, a fundamental doctrine of Christianity. They refer to this (& deifying Mary) as "polytheism" many times in the Quran. The specific Sonship of Christ (which is vital to Christianity) is squashed by outright denial. (Q.4:157). While Jesus Christ & Apostles stressed the sin problem & solution, there is little mention of sins by the Quran except such as Q.47:2 & 34 where it says believe in Muhammad & get sins removed. Jesus Christ said, "unless you believe that I am He (the Messiah), you will die in your sin." John 8:24. Then Jews & Christians are clearly said to be "wrongdoers". Q.5:51 (there's that political root.)

The copy of the Quran I have, has a very interesting introduction which is high-minded but misleading. It says the message has "nothing to do with violence", only peace. But Q. 4:56 & 89 say "to the fire . . . seize them & kill them . . .", and other references to mayhem & smashing anyone who disbelieves their teachings, which is still happening today. The Christian way is <u>drastically different</u> – it teaches forgiveness of adversaries, and "live in peace; and the God of love/peace shall be with you." 2 Corinthians 13:11. There are some real choice "pictures" of paradise in the Quran - Q.76:12-22, and other refs. of devotee's reward. And probably all Christians should read the Quran, but <u>also</u> all Muslims should read the New Testament. But I understand the <u>political blocker</u>. We generally cannot read theirs, and they generally cannot read ours.

Well I know we all believe what we WANT to believe (a Mormon told me this). I personally want to go with the root of Moses, David, the Messiah Jesus Christ, the Apostles, & God's revealed plan of salvation which is wonderful & <u>pre-dates Islam by 600 years</u>. "Thus says the Lord, Stand by the roads, and look, and ask for the ancient paths, where the good way is; and walk in it, and find rest for your souls." Jeremiah 6:16 And the <u>Messiah Jesus Christ</u> came for Cornelius & Arabs & everyone else. That's what the Acts 10 incident is all about. Choose Jesus, He is Alive. Muhammad is still in his grave. See also "I Saw the King" note 7.

PHYSICAL SENSES & 5 OTHERS

They say that humans have five physical senses: They are Sight, Hearing, Smell, Taste, and Touch. It's these amazing abilities that greatly help us humans to interact with our world. But nearly all animals also have the same five senses. Shouldn't the human being "created in the image of God" have extra or Other senses also?? Of course, we do. Humans also have at least five senses of the Soul & Spirit. They are Reason, Imagination, Memory, Conscience, and the Heart stuff – Affections & Emotions:

- Reason – how about that famous French statue (Le Penseur 1901) of a man sitting with elbow on knee, & head resting on his fist deep in thought. Animals might think a little, but they don't think a lot – (typically animals don't worry much either like we do.)
- Imagination – Unger's Bible Dictionary; "It's the image-making, pictorial faculty of the mind . . . It illustrates, adorns, and illuminates our speech and writing by presenting new views . . . It is the artist's great qualification . . ."
- Memory – According to Webster; the power, act, or process of recalling to mind facts previously learned or past experiences. Young people typically take this for granted, while older folks can be in real trouble here.
- Conscience – Unger again; "Conscience is not so much a distinct faculty of the mind, like perception, memory, etc., . . . as (it is) employed with reference to moral truth. It implies moral sense "to discern both good and evil." (Hebrews 5:14 & 1 Timothy 4:2)
- Affections/Emotions – These are accompanied by strong feelings or trembling in the heart – opposed to Reason, which goes on in the head. A brief list of emotions could be love, hate, fear, gladness, sorrow, shame, anger, etc. – all of which flow from the heart, which is the "center" of the Soul & Spirit. And the pain of a broken heart is where too many dis-appointments with life & love have left one with a damaged Soul & Spirit. In fact, that is when a lot of people entertain thoughts of suicide or turn to God.

So, what's the point of this "Gospel Note". Just this – humans should be grateful for the five additional senses beyond what animals have. We should acknowledge those senses of the Soul & Spirit as coming from Above. We should nourish & cultivate those Divine senses & not abuse them living in "youthful passions" and sin. The best way I know (from experience & about 50 years of study), is to be Born Again (John 3:3) & Transformed by God's power (Romans 12:2). God's salvation is an enhancer/expander of those senses of the Soul & Spirit. But denying that salvation can stunt the growth & control of those Other senses. What a waste of the most beautiful part of humanness.

- Genesis 1:27 "So God created man in his own image, in the image of God he created him; male and female he created them."
- Job 32:8-9 "It is the spirit in a man, the breath of the Almighty, that makes him understand. It is not the old that are wise, nor the aged that understand what is right."
- Psalms 5:12 "For thou dost bless the righteous, O Lord; thou dost cover him with favor as with a shield." (That blessing itself is an enhancer of the senses of Soul & Spirit.)
- John 3:3 "Truly, truly, I say to you, unless one is born anew, he cannot see the kingdom of God."
- Romans 12:2 "Do not be conformed to this world but be transformed by the renewal of your mind, that you may prove what is the will of God, what is good and acceptable and perfect."
- 2 Timothy 2:22 "So shun youthful passions and aim at righteousness, faith, love, and peace, along with those who call upon the Lord from a pure heart."

Choose Jesus, He is Alive. And one of the questions we may hear from a Big Voice on Judgment Day is this, "What did you do with your extra senses??" It will feel good to answer, "I used them wisely, Sir." See also "What's in The Blood?" note 96.

195

WHY IS THERE EVIL?

This is a question that many have asked for a long time. And of course, it is a religious question. If God is good, and all powerful, why does He allow evil to hurt so many innocent people? On the small scale we see a drunk driver who walks away from the accident, while the other car's occupants go to the morgue. Then we have crazies with guns shooting numerous people for sport, and crazies with cars running over numerous people for an ideology. Then we have Hollywood promoting evil for money by producing horrible sin & killing intensive flics for us to emulate. On the grand scale we have millions of innocents dying in wars from the beginning of time. I'll briefly touch the answer of 3 religions, (but for birth defects & disease & famine, only God has the answer.)

In Buddhism evil is a part of life. There needs to be evil to illustrate good. How can good exist without it's opposite? For the American Indian, evil is caused by evil spirits. They have no explanation where the spirits came from, but there are spells to placate evil spirits, so they stay away. The Judeo-Christian view is much more elaborate and, in my experience, & opinion, more credible.

God is the creator of the spiritual dimension AND its occupants – angels. There are only a few named "top management" angels such as Gabriel, Michael, & Lucifer (who may have been the highest ranking), then possibly millions of "worker bee" angels. Before time as we know it, a conspiracy happened in that dimension above, BECAUSE God gives FREE WILL & Lucifer was condemned along with his following for trying to take God's position, (see Isaiah 14:12-17, Ezekiel 28:12-17)

Then we have the "very good" physical creation – earth, animals, man, etc. The most perfect place was for the perfect man & woman, and they had perfect reproductive systems. But man & woman had FREE WILL and transgressed God's command (by the lie & luring of that serpent Lucifer). Paradise lost… Now that original couple were the representatives & SEED of the human race. We were evicted from the perfect place, lost a perfect relationship w/God, AND sent out into a "cursed" world with a fallen nature to multiply like flies. And sin/evil has been in this imperfect world since then, along with all the suffering, sickness, uncertainty, & death. "Many have wondered: Is evil so big that God cannot destroy it? If good cannot exist without its wicked twin, have we found a chink in God's all-powerful armor? Is there something God can't do?" (from The Religion Book, 2004 Jim Willis) My answer is NO. God can do anything He wants. The real question is: Why does God allow evil? I believe He uses evil to test us. This life is a proving ground of human character & affiliation - which side are we choosing - the narrow path of good & God, or the wider path of rebellion & pride/ego & going with the god of this world. And God has generously given the Bible & ministers/priests to give us light and answers if we choose to accept those answers. Some Bible refs. may be helpful:

- Genesis 1:1 & 31a "In the beginning God created the heavens and the earth. . . And God saw everything that he had made, and behold, it was very good."
- Genesis 3:17 & 19 "And to Adam he said, "Because you have listened to the voice of your wife, and have eaten of the tree of which I commanded you, 'You shall not eat of it,' cursed is the ground because of you; in toil you shall eat of it all the days of your life; . . . In the sweat of your face you shall eat bread till you return to the ground, for out of it you were taken; you are dust, and to dust you shall return."
- Romans 5:12 "Sin came into the world through one man and death through sin, and so death spread to all men because all men sinned."
- James 4:2 "You desire and do not have; so you kill. And you covet and cannot obtain; so you fight and wage war. You do not have, because you do not ask."
- Revelation 12:9 "And the great dragon was thrown down, that ancient serpent, who is called the Devil and Satan, the deceiver of the whole world - he was thrown down to the earth, and his angels were thrown down with him." (And demons possess people still today - see "Demon Possession", note 168.)
- Psalms 23:4 "Even though I walk through the valley of the shadow of death, I fear no evil; for thou art with me; thy rod and thy staff, they comfort me." (There is peace & hope in "relationship".)

Christ came into the world to give hope & salvation, from the spirit of sin/evil in the world & in ourselves. It requires faith & seeking, but it will pay off, because Jesus defeated evil & paid for our sin on the cross. So, we can also defeat evil & have restored relationship w/God, and ultimately Paradise regained - for eternity, and no evil will be there. That's the Gospel (good news) message, and the answer to the question of evil. Choose Jesus, He is Alive. "And there is salvation in no one else, for there is no other name under heaven given among men by which we must be saved." Acts 4:12 See also "Human Nature" note 182.

196

WHAT IS THE GOSPEL?*

There are major themes in the Bible such as God, faith, the kingdom, hell, the Gospel, etc. Well, the word "Gospel" is something mentioned often by Christ & the Apostles. And if 20 people were asked what the Gospel is, we would get 20 different answers.

Basically, Gospel means good news. It reveals penetrating truth from Divine quarters about: 1) God & His nature, 2) about man, 3) about how Jesus Christ fits into the picture, then 4) OUR response. Since the Apostle Paul is the "brains" of the New Testament, his inspired letters of Scripture are helpful in this analysis of the Gospel.

1. The clearest "nutshell" glimpse of God's nature is way back in the time of Moses where God is said to be compassionate & gracious & patient & one to forgive. But He does not leave the guilty unpunished. Sin has to be dealt with. Exodus 34:6-7 (God is not like a lazy janitor who sweeps dirt under rugs, furniture, etc.) We are accountable to Him – "we are created, we are made, therefore we are owned".[17] Greg Gilbert
2. Paul explains clearly (by Divine inspiration) that all humans, Jews & others have rebelled. Going back to the BEGINNING we (in Adam) rejected God's authority & declared our independence – a conspiracy against the King. (Lucifer's fall was similar – see note 195 "Why Is There Evil?")
3. God's "good news" solution to humanity's fatal sin problem is the sacrificial suffering, death & resurrection of Jesus Christ. No other savior dies for our sin problem, then rises from the dead. The resurrection seals & verifies the sacrifice of Christ, and the Apostles were energized by this. Then we have the doctrine of substitution. G. Gilbert put it this way; "when we put our faith in Jesus, we are relying on him to stand as our substitute before God, in both his perfect life and his penalty–paying death for us on the cross . . . we are trusting that God will substitute Jesus' record for ours, and declare us to be righteous (Romans 3:22)[18] . . . it is only the fully human, fully Divine Son of God who can save us."[19]
4. OUR response/action is to repent from sin & believe in Jesus. This is what the Apostles (starting with Peter) called people to do. And Christ & the Apostles used the word "saved". So, from what?? From sin & it's

consequences which are separation from God & His goodies in life & eternity. See "What is Saved?" note 39 (And a lot of folks – even in the church – are not saved according to Jesus Christ . . . "I never knew you." Matthew 7:21-23.)

The following refs. may be appropriate for this essay:

- Exodus 34:6-7 "The Lord passed before him, and proclaimed, "The Lord, the Lord, a God merciful and gracious, slow to anger, and abounding in steadfast love and faithfulness, keeping steadfast love for thousands, forgiving iniquity and transgression and sin, but who will by no means clear the guilty, visiting the iniquity of the fathers upon the children and the children's children, to the third and the fourth generation." (God's nature)
- Romans 1:16 "For I am not ashamed of the gospel: it is the power of God for salvation to everyone who has faith, to the Jew first and also to the Greek."
- Romans 4:24-25 "It will be reckoned to us who believe in him that raised from the dead Jesus our Lord, who was put to death for our trespasses and raised for our justification."
- 1 Corinthians 15:3-5 "For I delivered to you as of first importance what I also received, that Christ died for our sins in accordance with the Scriptures, that he was buried, that he was raised on the third day in accordance with the Scriptures, and that he appeared to Cephas (Peter), then to the twelve."

It appears that people often want a "center" or "focus" in religion (or Christianity) that is something other than the death of Jesus on the cross in the place of us sinners. But Paul makes it clear there is not another way. "As we have said before, so now I say again, If anyone is preaching to you a gospel contrary to that which you received, let him be accursed." Galatians 1:9 And I should apologize if some of my other gospel-notes don't make this clear enough . . . Choose Jesus, and His Gospel, They are "Alive". For the other side of the coin see "Liberal Theology" note 161.

* This essay is based on a recent book by one Greg Gilbert – same title. He did a great job worthy to be condensed.

197

ISM'S IN THE WAY

Not long ago I listened to a Romanian monk of a monastery explain about common blockers to the Christian faith. He mentioned only three: Marxism, Atheism, and Existentialism. But it would appear that the adversary of our souls has an "ISM" for nearly everybody. A quick look at the internet lists hundreds. Touching just a few:

- Egotism – an excessive self-focus. The belief that self-interest is the proper goal of all human actions.
- Existentialism -- "this represents a revolt against external authority, ready-made world views, authoritarian and conventional moral values and codes of conduct. Man has been dumped into the world whether he likes it or not. He has to make his own way in it, creating his own values . . ."[20] from Zondervan. Existentialism is a philosophical approach to life that condones our sin & selfishness. Some proponents are atheists while others profess Biblical faith (??).
- Gnosticism – "an early trend of religious thought . . . which flourished in the Hellenistic (Greek) Near East. There were numerous Gnostic sects, both pagan and Christian. The Christian Gnostics denied the literal meaning of the Scriptures and saw only an esoteric meaning based on gnosis, e.g. they did not believe that a real Jesus was really crucified." Webster's Encyclopedic Dictionary
- Hedonism – a belief that pleasure is the principal good in life.
- Humanism – a belief that humans are basically good at heart needing little or no Salvation and will ultimately solve all world problems by ambition & teamwork.
- Liberalism – in politics it's the philosophy that personal freedom & democratic government is supreme. In religion it broadly interprets the Bible & shuns rigid doctrine. See note 161 "Liberal Theology".
- Mysticism – getting spiritual truths by fixed meditation, or through esoteric/occult rites & doctrines, etc. – Yoga is a common form, but does it open people to demon influence?? See note 43 "The Demon"

Well most of the above ISM's appeal to thinking type folks. But there are plenty of ISM's for the rest of us also. And of course, we have thousands of "other" religions to distract souls. I believe our adversary Lucifer has "covered all bases" making it REALLY a challenge to find our connection with the real God. Maybe something like "running the gauntlet" . . . BUT for those who desire the "real deal", God has given the record of Israel, and the New Testament Scriptures to provide genuine spiritual light. And Jesus is the brightest "star" of that light.

Jesus said, "I am the light of the world; he who follows me will not walk in darkness but will have the light of life." John 8:12 He also said, "I am the way, and the truth, and the life; no one comes to the Father, but by me." John 14:6 "There is a way which seems right to a man, but its end is the way to death." Proverbs 14:12 "Beware lest any man spoil you through philosophy and vain deceit, after the tradition of men, after the rudiments of the world, and not after Christ." Colossians 2:8 KJV "Truth shall forever be on the scaffold, and wrong forever on the throne as long as time shall last."[7] H. Lindsell "No road to perdition has ever been more thronged than that of false Doctrine. Error is a shield over the conscience, and a bandage over the eyes."[6] D.C. Hodge

Considering that each one of us has an eternal soul, it only makes sense to find the genuine Salvation of God. A "blocker" or a fake "bill of goods" is not what we need. Choose Jesus, He is Alive. "Behold I stand at the door and knock; if anyone hears my voice and opens the door, I will come in to him and eat with him, and he with me." Jesus Christ Revelation 3:20, see also "Rude Surprises" note 79.

198

PERSECUTION

This is a subject that is negative, and it is very old in this world. It could be said that Cain persecuted Able – extremely. David the king wrote MUCH about Persecution in the Psalms. Jeremiah was considered the "Weeping Prophet" for (national decline) & the attacks on his character he suffered. Jesus the Christ was seriously (and fatally) persecuted. Paul the "grafted in" Apostle was possibly the MOST persecuted of all Apostles. (see 2 Corinthians 11:23-27) Most Christians of the first couple centuries suffered <u>severe</u> persecutions by the Jews & especially Romans. (The Coliseum of Rome has a dark & murderous history.)

The definition of Persecution is actually simple – even in Webster's Encyclopedic Dictionary: "to cause to suffer, esp. for religious or political reasons; to vex or harass." And that suffering varies <u>greatly</u>, depending when & where the "sufferee" is in history. The usual kind of persecution for the Christian in today's free world is mild (in most cases), but it can be very hard to deal with. Yes, we can find that spiritual "connection" with Jesus Christ & it may be real & life changing. The problem arises when those around us – family, friends, work associates, etc. find fault with our faith, and actively oppose us & our Christian Value system. As Christ Himself was opposed, so His followers must expect rejection, and being hated for His sake. While it's rare today to be killed, it's common to be laughed at & insulted, and ostracized in social groups we value. And termination from work is common also. I would venture to say most new Christians who have made a real stand for Christ, & then quit the Christian Life do so because of Persecution.

Why is there persecution? <u>One reason is</u> Group Psychology – going contrary to the "herd" instinct. Can you imagine a lemming going the wrong way – his furry little friends would find fault with him. Us humans also have a herd instinct & those who challenge the "norms" will be punished. <u>Another reason is</u> Logic. If creationists are right, then Darwinism is wrong which rubs the big bang & evolutionist folks "the wrong way". And today's political correctness bashes anything conservative, and considers it retarded. <u>Another reason is</u> Spiritual. The god of this world has sway on the thinking of unsaved people. (This is hard to swallow, but it is the entire message of the New Testament – Acts 26:18.) Born Again folks "smell" different in the "nostrils" of those who think Born Again is a fantasy or a farce. (See 2 Corinthians 2:15-16 below.) Another reason is Prophetic. Jesus said we would be persecuted, and He wasn't a man to lie . . .

Who claiming Jesus Christ, doesn't get persecuted? Well Robinson Caruso didn't worry about it much. There are a few who join monasteries to get away from Persecution. And I believe a host of good-hearted religious folks wax liberal in doctrine, so they won't have to face Persecution. But what does the Book say about it?

- Psalms 119:51 "Godless men utterly deride me, but I do not turn away from thy law."
- V. 69 "The godless besmear me with lies, but with my whole heart I keep thy precepts;"
- Psalms 120:7 "I am for peace; but when I speak, they are for war!" King David
- Matthew 10:16-17 "Behold, I send you out as sheep in the midst of wolves; so be wise as serpents and innocent as doves. Beware of men; for they will deliver you up to councils and flog you in their synagogues."
- John 15:19 "If you were of the world, the world would love its own; but because you are not of the world, but I chose you out of the world, therefore the world hates you." - the words of Jesus Christ.
- 2 Corinthians 2:15-16 "For we are the aroma of Christ to God among those who are being saved and among those who are perishing, to one a fragrance from death to death, to the other a fragrance from life to life."
- 2 Timothy 3:12-13 "Indeed all who desire to live a godly life in Christ Jesus will be persecuted, while evil men and impostors will go on from bad to worse, deceivers and deceived."

Well, I personally know it can be tough to make a stand with the Lord in this world today. But maybe the elements of Christianity are screeners that God uses to test our character. Elements like repentance, attending a legitimate church, prayer, giving, forgiving others, and of course PERSECUTION. It's ALL a part of it. And as we approach the end, & the Lord's soon return, persecution will positively get worse. (It may incur martyrdom to identify with Jesus Christ during the Great Tribulation – see Revelation 12:11.) The bottom line is something like this: "Suffer with Christ and for Christ, if you desire to reign with Christ."[21] Thomas A Kempis. Choose Jesus, He is Alive. See also "Human Nature" note 182.

199

THE HEATHEN – HOW LOST?

With today's political correctness & New Age thought in the air, it is almost taboo to think anyone is lost in God's "ever loving" eyes. Let's begin with a definition of Heathen: (from Webster's Encyclopedic Dictionary) – a person who does not worship the God of the Jews, Christians, or Muslims*. The same dictionary says pagans are similar to heathens. And of course, the "bleeding heart" & intellectual mind today is offended to hear that all but Judeo/Christian souls are lost. But going back 100+ generations, some patriarchs of heathen/pagan groups went in the wrong direction from revealed Biblical truth. It's been available all over the world B.C. & especially A.D. Many lands just didn't want that Biblical truth – (doctrine, traditions, or destiny).

It's not reasonable to expect Almighty God to change His revealed Biblical standards of lost & saved just because mankind tends to go astray and stay in darkness. For thousands of years missionaries have been sent to all lands with the Gospel of Christ. And many have been persecuted & killed by heathen/pagan folks as nearly all Christ's apostles were because of the Gospel message. What more could God have done to get the good news of Christ's salvation & resurrection out to the people of the world? Could or should He write the Gospel in the clouds?? No – the message "only Jesus saves" is spread by preaching, and/or by word of mouth. It's just God's way. (And for the question of those remote souls that never got the "word" of Messiah Christ & His saving work, see "Common Conundrums" note 100.)

Now, looking at the question of how lost are the Heathen from a logical point of view (common computer logic – IF, THEN, ELSE), we can confidently say: IF the Scriptures are truly of God, THEN heathen should go by what they say. IF the Scriptures are not genuine, ELSE – anything goes. I am persuaded God's Scripture is true & provides: 1) Knowledge of God & the Gospel message, 2) How to maintain legitimate spiritual life, & 3) Certain knowledge of God's will. BUT, how do modern day heathens determine those 3 soul-saving things if they have no preacher or Bible, or they have been led to believe the Bible is false & no good?? They don't . . . and darkness continues. For no extra charge, here are a few refs. that may apply to this essay:

- Ezra 8:22b "The hand of our God is for good upon all that seek him, and the power of his wrath is against all that forsake him." - 480 years B.C. -

- Mark 8:38 "For whoever is ashamed <u>of me and of my words</u> in this adulterous and sinful generation, of him will the Son of man also be ashamed, when he comes in the glory of his Father with the holy angels." - The words of Christ.
- John 14:6 "I am the way, and the truth, and the life; no one comes to the Father, but by me."
- Acts 4:12 "And there is salvation in no one else, for there is no other name under heaven given among men by which we must be saved." - Peter preaching to the lost of 1st century.
- 1 Corinthians 15:3 "For I delivered to you <u>as of first importance</u> what I also received, that Christ died for our sins in accordance with the Scriptures." (Paul›s word to the Corinthians.)
- Ephesians 2:12-13 ". . . you were at that time separated from Christ, alienated from the commonwealth of Israel, and strangers to the covenants of promise, having no hope and without God in the world. But now in Christ Jesus you who once were far off have been brought near in the blood of Christ." (Paul's word to the Ephesian heathens.)
- Galatians 1:8 "But even if we, or an angel from heaven, should preach to you a gospel contrary to that which we preached to you, let him be accursed." - Inspiration of Apostle Paul -

Looking at the title question <u>from a Scripture point of view</u>, it's clear the heathen are totally lost. And I am aware how totally PNC** this is today. (It's why liberals slide away from literal interpretation of the Bible.) But I personally prefer to be safe rather than sorry. And I did hear Christ's voice say, "Learn of Me", which is a quote of Matthew 11:29. He <u>verified</u> the Scriptures to me, so I write . . . (See note 7 "I Saw the King"). If you feel more like a Heathen/pagan than a Born-Again child of God, it's easy to change. Choose Jesus, He is Alive. Find a Bible believing church and connect. Lots of former Heathens will be there. See also "Other Gods" note 188.

* While it may be the same God, Jews & Muslims generally reject Christ & New Testament truth. Muslims persecute & KILL Christian Missionaries today as they always have.
** PNC -- Politically NOT Correct.

200

IN WHAT DO WE TRUST?

This country's roots started about 1492, and in the parameters of faith it produced our founders & our constitution. "In God We Trust" has been on our money for the better part of a century. Nearly all of our schools & churches & courts held to Bible standards of religion, truth & justice, work ethic, man & woman marriage, etc... We Americans trusted in this value system for about 475 years. And it has produced phenomenal growth & progress and saved the world from various international threats. But NOW what do we trust in??

- Friends & social group – it's almost religious how folks hold these.
- Self & ego, youth & beauty – mostly according to Hollywood patterns.
- Coffee??, alcohol, & devious drugs – the American mind is altercated . . .
- Political Correctness – defined as avoiding any kind of speech or writing that would offend those groups who have a "special" agenda or value system, such as civil rights, LGBT rights, feminism, and environmental causes. P.C. seems to ram something down our throats contrary to personal freedom, & the "majority rules" fabric of this democracy.
- Education & Science – man's thinking is embraced as supreme.
- Money – even though losing the gold standard has ruined the value of the dollar by 90% in the last 70 years.
- Computers, addictive video games & instant commo. is/are the new "holy".
- Expensive medical & medicines – other leading countries have MUCH less costly medical.
- Universal salvation – as in New Age (#56) & Other Gods (#188), which the Bible does <u>not</u> support – that "light" at the end of the tunnel may well be a "train" - (Lucifer & hell). 2 Corinthians 11:14 ". . . even Satan disguises himself as an angel of light."

I believe the shift in the U.S. value system, and the drastic re-set from traditional Godly orientations is due in part to <u>Deconstruction</u>. That is "the notion that language is a hopelessly imperfect vehicle for the expression of ideas, and because words have no inherent meaning, "meaning" – all meaning – is relative . . ." David Thibodaux * Deconstruction is a philosophical theme which has been brewing in our universities for over

50 years. And guess what Book it especially targets . . .? Our adversary the devil is delighted to see it undermine our Judeo/Christian culture. We see the result of this devious thinking in our SCHOOLS, political parties, courts, organized anarchy endorsed by liberal governors, liberal churches, even families – NOTHING appears to be holy anymore . . . Some Scripture refs. that may apply:

"If the foundations are destroyed, what can the righteous do?" (Psalms 11:3) "Blessed is the man who makes the Lord his trust, who does not turn to the proud, to those who go astray after false gods!" (Psalms 40:4) "He who despises the word brings destruction on himself, but he who respects the commandment will be rewarded." (Proverbs 13:13) "He who trusts in his own mind is a fool; but he who walks in wisdom will be delivered." (Proverbs 28:26) "An appalling and horrible thing has happened in the land; the prophets prophesy falsely, and the priests rule at their direction; my people love to have it so, but what will you do when the end comes?" (Jeremiah 5:30-31) "But he who takes refuge in me shall possess the land, and shall inherit my holy mountain." (Isaiah 57:13b)

I realize from history that maybe the biggest challenge to the human race is to simply hang on to what is true & good. Like the Bible & "In God We Trust". But it's sad to witness today's value shift. And especially sad is knowing that American people are classically ripe candidates for judgment & hell because of the Godly truth & traditions of the Judeo/Christian heritage that's been here for over 500 years. (Hebrews 6:4-8). I would like to see a national revival & change in direction (before we lose this good country). That "change" must start with the individual – like you & me. Choose Jesus, He is Alive. That gives "In God We Trust" real meaning. See also "The Eagle", note 50.

* Political Correctness, David Thibodaux, PHD, pg. 20, 1992

EPILOGUE

Solomon, son of King David offers these "closing thoughts":

"Remember now your Creator in the days of your youth, Before the difficult days come, And the years draw near when you say, "I have no pleasure in them"

"And further, my son, be admonished by these. Of making many books there is no end, and much study is wearisome to the flesh. Let us hear the conclusion of the whole matter: Fear God, and keep his commandments, For this is man's all. For God will bring every work into judgment, Including every secret thing, Whether good or evil." NKJV Ecclesiastes 12:1, 12-14

Then back to the Gospel Notes book title - AN ATHEIST SAID, . . . "There is one thing that mars all the pleasure of my life; I am afraid the Bible is true. If I could only know for a certainty that death is an eternal sleep, I should be happy. But here is what pierces my soul: if the Bible is true, I am lost forever!" [22]

"The fool hath said in his heart, There is no God" (Psalm 14:1).

--Shaw, Dying Testimonies of Saved and Unsaved[22]

BIBLIOGRAPHY

[1] Mark Twain Quotes. BrainyQuote.com. Retrieved July 16, 2020, from BrainyQuote.com https//www.brainyquote.com/quotes/mark_twain_153869

[2]South, Dr. John, A Journey Through PTSD, LifeGuide Press, 2015

[3] Stuart Hamblen 1951

[4] Fields, W.C., "Fields for President", 1943, chapter 7; Taylor Trade Publishing

[5] "Mother Teresa Quotes." BrainyQuote.com. BrainyMedia Inc, 2020. 18 July 2020. https://www.brainyquote.com/quotes/mother_teresa_131833

[6] Hodge, Charles, "Commentary on the Epistle to the Romans"; Wm. B. Eerdman Publishing, Grand Rapids, MI

[7]Lindsell, Harold, "Battle For The Bible", 1976, Zondervan Publishing

[8]. Tomczak, Larry, Divine Appointments:Igniting Your Passion to Fulfill Your Destiny, Destiny Image Publishers, 1998

[9] Bright, Dr. Bill, "Jesus Gives Power for Living, The Secret Is Surrender", New Life Publications, 1971,1998

[10] Freud, Sigmund 1856-1939, "Letters To Ferenczi"

[11] Boettner, Loraine, "The Inspiration of Scripture", Part 1-6, Conclusion; Reformed.org, copyright 1996-2020

[12] Pink, Arthur W., Divine Inspiration Of The Bible, Chapter 10, Bible Truth Depot Publishers and Booksellers, copyright 1917

[13] Huxley, Aldous, "Collected Essays", Published by Harper Colophon, 1971 (first published 1923)

[14] "James Callaghan Quotes." BrainyQuote.com. BrainyMedia Inc, 2020. 10 August 2020. https://www.brainyquote.com/quotes/james_callaghan_205196

[15] Hitler, Adolf, "Mein Kampf", 1925; originally taken from Chapter 10 of James Murphy's translation of Mein Kampf (the quote is one paragraph in Murphy›s translation and in the German original)

[16] Brands, H.W., Author & History Professor at University of Texas; Lincoln Chronicles: Dark Night of the Soul, Historynet.com, American History, Oct. 2009

[17] Gilbert, Greg, What Is The Gospel? pg. 28

[18] Gilbert, Greg, What Is The Gospel? pg. 76

[19] Gilbert, Greg, What Is The Gospel? pg. 61-62

[20] The New International Dictionary of the Christian Church, pg. 365, copyright 1974

[21]Kempis, Thomas A. (Thomas Haemerken, monk), The Imitation of Christ, Book two "The Interior Life", Chapter 1 "Meditation". 1420's

[22] Myers, John, Voices from the Edge of Eternity, Whitaker House, 1968, 2012, page 71

www.ingramcontent.com/pod-product-compliance
Lightning Source LLC
Chambersburg PA
CBHW021153110726
47900CB00002B/555

* 9 7 8 0 5 7 8 7 7 2 4 5 5 *